The **Ready-Set-Read** *program*
*is proudly sponsored by:*

# King County
# Library System
# Foundation

*For more information on library services*
*and programs for children, please visit*
**www.kcls.org**

# The Promise

Greg watched and listened as the children sang Pakistan's national anthem to start their school day. He saw Twaha's seven-year-old daughter, Jahan, standing tall and straight beneath her headscarf as she sang. When the song ended, they sat down in the dirt and began writing out their multiplication tables. A few, like Jahan, had slates on which they wrote with sticks dipped in mud. The rest scratched in the dirt with sticks. "Can you imagine a fourth-grade class in America, alone, without a teacher, sitting there quietly and working on their lessons?" Greg asked later. "I felt like my heart was being torn out. . . . I knew I had to do something."

But what could he do? He had barely enough money left to travel by jeep and bus to Pakistan's capital, where he would catch an airplane to fly home. Still, there had to be something.

Standing next to Haji Ali, looking at the mountains that he'd come halfway around the world to climb, Greg suddenly felt that reaching the summit of K2 to place a necklace there wasn't really important. He could do something much better than that to honor his sister, Christa. He put his hands on Haji Ali's shoulders. "I *will* build a school," he said. "I promise."

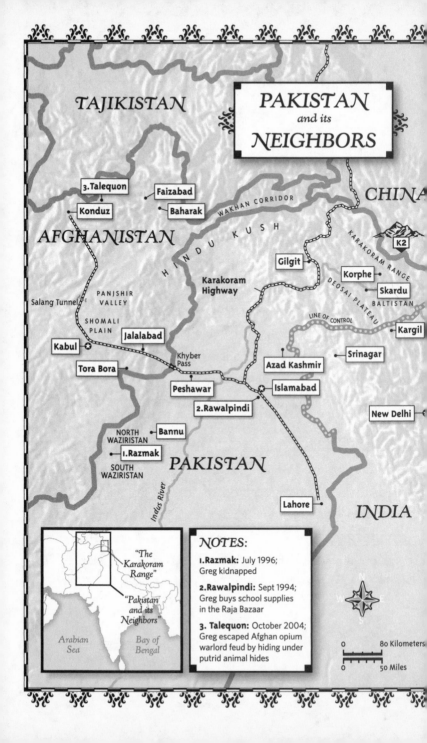

PAKISTAN
and its
NEIGHBORS

TAJIKISTAN

CHINA

3.Talequon
Faizabad
Konduz
Baharak

AFGHANISTAN

WAKHAN CORRIDOR

HINDU KUSH

KARAKORAM RANGE

K2

Gilgit

Korphe

Karakoram
Highway

DEOSAI PLATEAU

Skardu

BALTISTAN

PANJSHIR
VALLEY

Salang Tunnel

SHOMALI
PLAIN

Jalalabad

LINE OF CONTROL

Kargil

Kabul

Khyber
Pass

Azad Kashmir

Srinagar

Tora Bora

Peshawar

Islamabad

2.Rawalpindi

New Delhi

NORTH
WAZIRISTAN

Bannu

1.Razmak

PAKISTAN

SOUTH
WAZIRISTAN

Indus River

Lahore

INDIA

"The
Karakoram
Range"

"Pakistan
and its
Neighbors"

Arabian
Sea

Bay of
Bengal

NOTES:

1.Razmak: July 1996;
Greg kidnapped

2.Rawalpindi: Sept 1994;
Greg buys school supplies
in the Raja Bazaar

3. Talequon: October 2004;
Greg escaped Afghan opium
warlord feud by hiding under
putrid animal hides

0       80 Kilometers

0       50 Miles

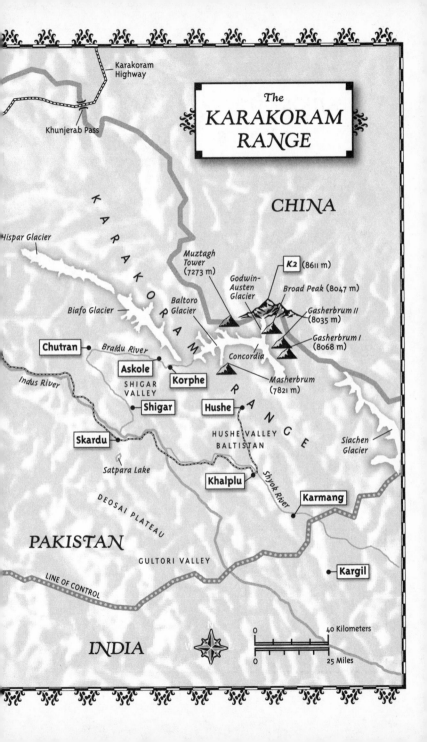

# Three Cups of Tea

## Young Readers Edition

Greg Mortenson and David Oliver Relin

Adapted for young readers by
Sarah Thomson

*Dial Books for Young Readers*

DIAL BOOKS FOR YOUNG READERS
Published by the Penguin Group
Penguin Young Readers Group, 345 Hudson Street, New York, New York 10014, U.S.A.
Penguin Group (Canada), 90 Eglinton Avenue East, Suite 700, Toronto,
Ontario, M4P 2Y3 Canada (a division of Pearson Penguin Canada Inc.)
Penguin Books Ltd, 80 Strand, London WC2R 0RL, England
Penguin Ireland, 25 St Stephen's Green, Dublin 2, Ireland
(a division of Penguin Books Ltd)
Penguin Group (Australia), 250 Camberwell Road, Camberwell, Victoria 3124, Australia
(a division of Pearson Australia Group Pty Ltd)
Penguin Books India Pvt Ltd, 11 Community Centre,
Panchsheel Park, New Delhi - 110 017, India
Penguin Group (NZ), 67 Apollo Drive, Rosedale, North Shore 0632, New Zealand
(a division of Pearson New Zealand Ltd)
Penguin Books (South Africa) (Pty) Ltd, 24 Sturdee Avenue,
Rosebank, Johannesburg 2196, South Africa

Registered Offices: Penguin Books Ltd, 80 Strand, London WC2R 0RL, England

Published in the United States of America by Dial Books for Young Readers,
a division of Penguin Young Readers Group, 2009
Published simultaneously by Puffin Books, a division of Penguin Young Readers Group, 2009

5 7 9 10 8 6 4

LIBRARY OF CONGRESS CATALOGING-IN-PUBLICATION DATA IS AVAILABLE

Dial Books For Young Readers ISBN 978-0-8037-3392-3

Pennies for Peace™ is a trademark of Central Asia Institute.
Printed in the United States of America

# ACKNOWLEDGMENTS

We hope you enjoy the young readers edition of *Three Cups of Tea* and it inspires you to go out and make a difference in your city, town, country, or around the world. It has been incredibly exciting to work with Puffin to create the young readers edition, and to listen and respond to your requests to make it a better learning experience by adding maps, a glossary, Who's Who, a time line, photos, and more.

First of all, thanks to all the dedicated teachers, workers, staff and dedicated communities and children in Pakistan and Afghanistan, who have given everything so that their children can learn to read and write and attend school.

Thank you to all the teachers all over the world, who dedicate their lives to education. You are our heroes, who constantly inspire, motivate, and give children the light of hope for the future.

Thanks to librarians who promote literacy and books, and help guide us with access to knowledge and information.

Thanks to David Oliver Relin, the coauthor of *Three Cups of Tea*, who worked hard for two years to get this story told. David's wife, Dawn, an elementary school teacher, was also a source of inspiration for this book.

Thank you Sarah Thomson (and your two cats), who from a small room in Maine adapted and wrote the superb young readers edition (her twentieth book).

Thanks to Paul Slovak, the Penguin editor of the adult version, who has been a constant source of support for *Three Cups of Tea* and who helped encourage it to be written in a young readers edition.

Thank you Eileen Kreit, publisher of Puffin, for your amazing energy and enthusiasm that never stops ("Go Girl!"), and for your extra interest and support  because of your own children.

A special thanks to Jen Bonnell, senior editor at Puffin, who worked patiently day and night for months to help get the book down and was a source of encouragement to Amira to share with her fellow students the experiences and feelings she has being a part of the *Three Cups of Tea* family. You rock!

Thanks also to the very dedicated people at the Penguin Young Readers Group, who helped with this book and also the Dial picture book, *Listen to the Wind,* including Deborah Kaplan, Lauri Hornik, Alisha Niehaus, Theresa Evangelista, Nick Vitiello, Teresa Kietlinski, and also Pat Shuldiner, who copyedited and proofed the book.

Thank you to Dr. Jane Goodall and the Roots & Shoots organization for the foreword, and for inspiring all of us to realize that all life is sacred, which we should cherish and protect.

Thanks to the humanitarian workers in the world, who work hard to help bring education, health, and environmental conservation to make our home, planet Earth, a better place. We also thank the peacemakers, and people serving in the military around the world, who also dedicate their lives to peace. Your sacrifices are always appreciated, and you are in our thoughts.

Thanks to my mother-in-law, Lila Bishop,  and her late husband,

Dr. Barry Bishop, who were both educators and instilled in us a love for geography and different cultures.

Thank you to all my cousins, extended family, and especially my sisters, Sonja Joy and Kari, brother-in-law Brent Bishop, and their spouses and children for blessing us with their love and strength of family.

Thanks to my mother, Jerene Mortenson, a lifelong educator, and my late father, Dempsey. From the time we were babies, they read books to us every night in Africa and taught us how important a life of service and education is.

Amira and Khyber, my two dear children, you are the angels in my life. It is never easy to have a father gone up to half of the year, for most of your childhood. You have given up many precious times we could have shared together—to read, play, explore life, and snuggle—so that other children could have hope through education. Your love and courage are the shining stars of our lives.

Lastly, thanks to my wife, Tara Bishop. You are a saint and love of my life. You are the rock that gives me hope and for which there are no words better to say than "I love you."

—Greg Mortenson

# Contents

Jane Goodall and Greg Mortenson

*Three Cups of Tea* is a fantastic book of adventure, courage, and determination. As you read it you will become increasingly amazed at how much one determined person can accomplish. It all began when Greg Mortenson lost his way up in the high mountains of Pakistan and was, just in time, rescued by his porter, Mouzafer. But Greg got lost again and wandered into a village. There, slowly, he recovered from the effects of exposure and got to know the people. He was horrified to find that there was no school. Imagine trying to learn from a teacher who comes only three days a week when you have no classroom and are sitting on the ground outside, often in freezing weather, and mostly without books and paper and pens. Greg made a promise that he would return and build a school.

Back in America almost no one believed in him or his mission, but finally he returned to Pakistan with enough money to honor his promise. This book describes the challenges he faced. Few people would have carried on against such daunting odds, surrounded by danger. (Indeed, he was kidnapped once, for eight terrifying days.) And few would have agreed to building other schools when, finally, the first one was completed. No wonder Greg Mortensen is a legendary figure in the remote villages where he works. Again and again he has risked his life in order to help the villagers educate their children.

The more I learned about this extraordinary man, the more I wanted to meet him. But as my schedule is always so full, and booked months in advance, and as Greg is so often traveling, I thought it would be a long time before this could happen. It seems, however, that we were meant to get together. For it happened that, within two months of finishing *Three Cups of Tea*, I was scheduled to give a talk in Bozeman, Montana, where Greg and his family live. And I had a few free hours and Greg was at home. And so it was that I found myself sitting and enjoying a cup of tea with Greg and his family—his wife, Tara, and their children, Amira and Khyber. And what a wonderful meeting it was. We had so much to talk about, including the years he had spent in Tanzania, where my team and I have been studying chimpanzees since 1960. Soon it seemed as though we had known each other for years.

Greg is a very big man: not only is he tall, but he has a huge heart. He is also very warm and gentle. He is the sort of person I admire most. He has achieved, and is achieving, marvelous things in Pakistan and, more recently, in Afghanistan, enabling children—especially girls who otherwise would have no chance to get educated—to learn about the world outside their villages. And Greg (helped now by his organization, the Central Asia Institute) is not only providing schools, he has gained the trust—and the hearts—of the people. This contributes more to world peace than misguided attempts to change the world through violence and war. Yet Greg, who has accomplished so much, is modest and unassuming.

We spent some time talking about the Jane Goodall Institute's youth program, Roots & Shoots (R&S). It is the perfect complement to the education provided for the children in the schools that Greg and his team are building, for it encourages young people, from preschool though university, to think about the problems around them, and then to take action to try to solve them. Members work to make this a better world for people, for animals, and for the environment. R&S began in Tanzania in 1991 and is now in nearly a hundred countries, and the nine thousand or so active groups are encouraged to make contact with one another, learn about one anothers' cultures, and share their hopes, their dreams. The most important message of R&S is that each one of us makes a difference every day. We must stop polluting Mother Earth and using up her natural resources. We must show respect for all living things. And we must learn how to live in peace and harmony within our families and our communities, and break down the barriers that divide people of different nationalities, cultures, and religions, and that exist between us and nature.

Amira knew about Roots & Shoots, and plans to start a group in her school. She told me she loves and respects animals and wild places. She told me about the "Pennies for Peace™" project, now in nearly two thousand schools—it is a perfect activity for R&S groups everywhere. Amira is determined to do her part in making the world a better place. She will help to introduce R&S not only in Montana, but maybe also in Pakistan and Afghanistan—for often Greg takes his family with him, to share the work, the excitement . . . and the danger. And Amira is a born leader.

We cannot all travel to Pakistan. Few people could do what Greg has done. But we can all, every one of us, make a difference in the world, every day. You can plant a tree, recycle, collect trash, care for an animal in need, give a penny for peace. You can learn about the problems faced by children in Pakistan and Afghanistan, and then perhaps you can find ways to communicate with them, to help them. And they, in turn, can learn about your culture and your problems. When we truly understand about people and their lives in other countries, when we write and receive letters from them, when we become friends, then the world becomes a happier and a safer place.

Thank you, Greg, for opening so many minds and hearts, for your courage, your determination, and your indomitable spirit. . . . And for attempting a seemingly impossible task—and succeeding in a way you cannot have predicted in the beginning. Your schools provide not only education, but hope for the future—for the future of the people you and your family have come to understand and love. Hope for the future of the world. Every brick in every school represents another step toward a more peaceful world.

Jane Goodall, Ph.D., DBE
Founder of The Jane Goodall Institute
UN Messenger of Peace
www.janegoodall.org
www.rootsandshoots.org

$A$*s-salaam alaikum!* Peace be with you! This is how over 1.3 billion Muslims greet each other around the world.

I want to thank you for picking up the young readers edition of *Three Cups of Tea*. I hope that my story inspires you and that it's fun to read and learn about children like you, who live in other countries and have different cultures, faiths, and traditions.

Reading and literacy are very important to me and my family. When I was growing up in Africa, my parents read bedtime stories to me and my sisters before we could even walk. It was our favorite time of day. Today, my wife, Tara, and I continue that tradition with our children, Amira and Khyber. We often go to the library with them to choose books.

But there are about 110 million children ages five to fifteen around the world who don't have a chance to learn how to read and write or to go to school. They can't get an education because of slavery, poverty, discrimination against girls, religious extremism, or corrupt governments. In India, some kids are forced to go out on the streets and beg for money. They're punished and beaten if they don't bring home enough at the end of the day. Some young people in Cambodia can't go to school because they have to work on rice farms. In China, thousands of children work in sweatshops making fireworks that we set off on the Fourth of July. West African boys and girls who aren't in school work on cocoa plantations, harvesting two million tons of cocoa that's used to make chocolate. In Africa, Asia, and South America, there are tens of thousands of children who have never been to school and are forced to become soldiers and learn to kill at a very young age. In Pakistan, thousands of illiterate children work sewing soccer balls; and in Afghanistan, many kids are forced to work in dimly lit rooms making carpets. Only their small fingers can weave the tiny knots that make up the expensive high-thread-count carpets that Westerners like to buy. Yet also in Pakistan and Afghanistan, some of the twenty-eight thousand students who go to the schools built by the Central Asia Institute will do anything for the privilege of going to school. Many walk two to three hours a day just to get an education.

Every child should have the right and privilege to have an education, as mandated in Article 26 of the United Nations Declaration of Human Rights. It's a big challenge to educate these children all over the world, but we should make it a top global priority. Ignorance breeds hatred, and the simplest way to stop that is to educate kids.

I believe that kids can make a difference, starting in your own schools and communities. One kid, and even just one penny, can help change the world. There are enough pennies in homes throughout the United States to be able to eliminate illiteracy completely throughout the world. If you want to do more, please check out the Pennies for Peace™ program and Jane Goodall's Roots & Shoots program. Through these programs, kids can learn how to help one another; promote peace; and make our communities, our countries, and our world better places.

—Greg Mortenson, January 2009

## A NOTE ON THE TEXT

Words printed in bold are included in
the glossary in the back of the book.

CHAPTER I
*Failure*

$G$reg Mortenson was lost.

He didn't know it yet.

He was hiking down the Baltoro **Glacier**, a frozen river that flows along a mountain slope at a rate of four inches a day. His heavy black boots didn't seem to be moving any faster than the ice beneath them. At any moment, he thought, he'd look up and see Scott Darsney, a fellow mountain climber, sitting on a rock, waiting and laughing at him for being so slow. But he didn't realize that he had taken a wrong turn. He should have been walking west, toward a village where he hoped to hire a jeep driver to take him out of the mountains. In reality, he was now headed south, into a landscape that was a maze of shattered chunks of ice.

Greg and Darsney were part of an **expedition** that had set out three months before to reach the **summit** of a mountain called K2, part of the **Karakoram** Range in Pakistan. K2 is the second-highest mountain on Earth; only Mount Everest reaches farther into the clouds. Most mountain climbers consider it to be the toughest peak in the world. Its slopes are so steep that snow can't cling to them. But Greg Mortenson knew what he was doing. He'd reached the summit of Mount **Kilimanjaro** by the age of eleven. He'd learned to climb in Yosemite National Park. He'd made it up mountains in the **Himalayas** before. He had no doubt that he'd reach the top of K2 with the **amber** necklace he carried in his pocket.

It had belonged to his sister, Christa, who'd died on her twenty-third birthday, in July 1992. Greg planned to leave the necklace on K2 in Christa's honor. And he'd come close— within six hundred feet of the summit. But now he was headed

Christa's amber neckace

Greg Mortenson (third from right in cap) with Scott Darsney (far right) before taking on K2

back down the mountain, Christa's necklace still in his pocket. Failure—not something he was used to—was on his mind.

Greg and Darsney had helped to rescue another member of their team, Etienne Fine. When Fine neared the summit of K2, he'd gotten extremely sick as fluid collected in his lungs, and tissues in his brain began to swell. This can happen to people at altitudes above what their bodies are used to. Along with the expedition's leaders, Dan Mazur and Jonathan Pratt, Greg and Darsney had carried Fine down the mountain to where a helicopter could land and take him to a hospital. Mazur and Pratt had returned and managed to reach the summit of K2, but Greg and Darsney, already exhausted from a stressful climb

3

earlier, had no strength left. Their only choice was to get down off the mountain as quickly as possible.

The human body doesn't function well in the high altitude of mountains like K2. Because air pressure drops as a climber gets higher, each breath takes in less oxygen. Operating on less oxygen than usual, people get headaches and feel weak, nauseated, and exhausted. They don't think clearly. Add in hard work and freezing temperatures, like those Greg had experienced on K2, and it's easy to become seriously weakened. Tasks that were once simple for a climber like Greg Mortenson—such as walking with a backpack full of climbing and camping gear—become almost impossible.

Greg had already lost thirty pounds in his attempt to climb K2. As he and Darsney made their way down to one of the base camps, where climbers prepared for their attempts to reach the summit, they found it took them hours to cover three miles. As they struggled, Greg and Darsney met Mouzafer Ali and his friend Yakub, two porters who made a living guiding and helping mountain climbers. They offered to carry the climbers' packs for four dollars a day. Greg and Darsney gladly agreed. Greg didn't know it at the time, but Mouzafer was known as one of the most skilled porters in the area.

But now, alone and walking down the Baltoro Glacier, all Greg knew was that he'd lost sight of Mouzafer as well as his friend. And Mouzafer was carrying the pack that held most of Greg's gear—his tent, his sleeping bag, his stove, his food, his flashlight, and his matches.

FAILURE

The sharp crack of a falling rock brought Greg's attention back to his surroundings. A boulder the size of a three-story house suddenly bounced down a slope and crushed an iceberg in front of him.

It was getting dark, and Greg's mind was fuzzy. He tried to think back to the last spot where he had glimpsed any sign of human beings. It had been hours since he'd seen Darsney. There were no signs that anyone had ever walked on the trail in front of him—no cigarette butts, no food tins, no droppings from the mules that were used to carry heavy loads. In fact, Greg realized, where he was walking didn't look much like a trail at all.

As the sun set, Greg spent an hour clambering up a slope of loose rock, hoping to get a view that would help tell him where he was. He knew of a landmark on another mountain, and if he could find it, he might be able to get his bearings. But when he got to the top of the slope, all he saw were unfamiliar peaks in the fading light. He had wandered about eight miles from where he should have been.

All he had with him was a small, purple backpack that held a blanket, an empty water bottle, and a single protein bar.

Greg was scared, and all alone. He knew that spending the night on this spot, even without his gear, would be less dangerous than stumbling over a glacier in the dark. He would have to wait and search for the trail in daylight. He found a flat slab of rock and wrapped himself in his blanket.

5

Then he filled his water bottle with snow, thawed his protein bar by holding it next to his skin, and ate it. Greg watched as the sun set behind the peaks that surrounded him, leaving him in darkness.

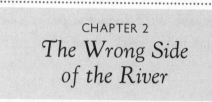

## CHAPTER 2
### The Wrong Side of the River

When Greg opened his eyes in the morning, he could barely breathe. He struggled to free his hands from the blanket wrapped around him and clawed at his face. Ice had frozen over his mouth and nose like a mask. He tore the ice free and was able at last to take a deep, satisfying breath.

He sat up and stretched. In the light before dawn, the mountain peaks were painted in sugary colors—pinks and purples and baby blues. The sky was clear, and there was no wind. Greg was still lost, still alone, and his hands were so stiff from the cold they were like claws. He couldn't even open his water bottle, half full of melted snow. But he wasn't worried. Morning made all the difference.

He was thinking more clearly, maybe because he'd managed to sleep a little. Now he could see that, if he walked for a few hours back the way he'd come, he would run into the trail he'd left. He set off north, stumbling over boulders and jumping over crevasses, deep cracks in the ice of the glacier. When he reached the top of a small crest, the sun finally rose over the walls of the valley around him.

Greg was stunned by the beauty of the peaks on every side. Gasherbrum, Broad Peak, Mitre Peak, Muztagh Tower—all these mountains, covered in ice, burned like bonfires in the raw light of the sun. Greg sat on a boulder and drank from his water bottle until it was empty. But he couldn't drink in enough of the sight before him. He'd been in these mountains for months, but that morning, it was as if he'd never seen them before. "In a way, I never had," he said later. "All summer, I'd looked at these mountains as goals, totally focused on the biggest one, K2. . . . But that morning, for the first time, I simply saw them. It was overwhelming."

He stumbled on. Even though he knew he had no food and no warm clothing and wouldn't survive if he didn't find both soon, he wasn't scared. He filled his water bottle from a melting trickle that ran from the glacier and winced from the cold as he drank. Food won't be a problem for days, he told himself, but you must remember to drink.

Late in the morning, he heard bells tinkling and realized that they were from a team of donkeys. The animals carried heavy loads to and from towns in the mountains. He tried to follow the bells but ran into a large rock wall that blocked the way. Greg realized that he'd gone too far. He must have walked over the trail without realizing it was there. Once again he turned and retraced his steps, this time looking down at the ground, not up at the breathtaking mountains. When he spotted a cigarette butt, then a pile of stones built to mark the trail, he realized he'd made it at last.

Then he spotted something else—someone standing on a boulder, silhouetted against the sky. Greg yelled and the man turned toward him, then jumped down and disappeared from his sight. Greg didn't have the strength to run, but he forced himself to trot toward the place where he'd seen the figure, yelling again and again. Finally he was close enough to see who the man was—Mouzafer, the porter he had hired to help carry his gear! Greg's heavy backpack was still on Mouzafer's back.

"Mr. Gireg, Mr. Gireg!" Mouzafer shouted, dropping the pack and wrapping Greg Mortenson in a bear hug. "**Allah Akbhar!** [God is great!] Blessings to **Allah** you're alive!"

Mouzafer let him go and began slapping him on the back in delight. Clouds of dust rose from Greg's clothes, and he doubled over, coughing. "*Cha*, Mr. Gireg," Mouzafer said, worried. "*Cha* will give you strength!"

**Paiyu cha** is a hot green tea, made with salt, baking soda, goat's milk, and an aged, sour butter churned from yak's milk. While it looks like chocolate milk, it doesn't taste like it. The **Balti**, Mouzafer's tribe who live in the high-altitude valleys in northern Pakistan, think of this butter as a delicacy. Greg, however, had smelled *paiyu cha* brewing many times and thought the odor was horrible. He describes it as "stinkier than the most frightening cheese the French ever invented." He'd come up with many different excuses to avoid drinking it.

Mouzafer lit a fire, brewed the tea, and stirred in the butter with a finger. Then he handed Greg a steaming mug. Greg gagged at the taste, but his body needed the hot liquid. He swallowed it. Mouzafer filled the mug two more times, and Greg drank it all.

For the next three days, until they were off the Baltoro Glacier, Mouzafer never let Greg out of his sight. He held his hand as they walked, or made Greg walk right behind him, his feet nearly touching the heels of Mouzafer's shoes. The porter, a devout **Muslim**, prayed five times a day, but even during his prayers he would glance up to make sure that Greg was still nearby.

Greg tried to learn some of the Balti language that Mouzafer spoke. Glacier was *gangs-zhing*, avalanche was *rdo-rut*. And there were many words for rocks. Small round rocks were *khodos*. *Brak-lep* was flat rock, good for sleeping or cooking on. *Khrok* was a wedge-shaped rock, excellent for sealing up holes in stone houses. Greg was good at languages. Soon he could communicate a little in Balti.

Finally Greg stepped off ice and onto solid ground for the first time in three months. From under the glacier, water shot out into a gorge and created the quick-moving Braldu River. Greg knelt down to look closely at a five-petaled pink rosehip, the first flower he'd seen in over eighty days, since his attempt to climb K2 began. Then he and Mouzafer began to walk along the riverbank.

Now that they were off the Baltoro Glacier, Mouzafer

thought it was safe enough to hike ahead and set up camp each day. Greg, walking more slowly on his tired and aching legs, stopped often to rest; but he always followed the river until he saw the smoke from Mouzafer's campfire in the evenings.

Seven days after leaving K2, Greg saw his first trees. The five poplars stood in a row, and so Greg knew they had been planted by people. He was back where human beings could live. The trees told Greg he'd made it down alive.

Looking at the poplars, Greg didn't see that the trail he was following had a fork. One path led down to the river, where it would eventually reach a bridge. The bridge led to Askole, the village Greg was headed for. But by mistake he took the other path, walking toward the trees. For the second time, he'd lost his way.

The poplars led into apricot orchards. Piles of the ripe fruit were stacked on hundreds of flat baskets. There were women kneeling by the baskets, splitting the fruit and setting aside the pits. When they saw Greg, they pulled their shawls over their faces and ran to put the trees between themselves and the stranger.

But the children were not so shy. As Greg kept walking into the fields planted with buckwheat and barley, children came up to touch his clothes and took turns holding his hands. For the first time in a while, Greg thought about what he looked like. It had been about three months since he'd had a shower. His hair was long and dirty. He felt huge and filthy, and he stooped, trying not to tower over the children. But they didn't seem to be scared of him. By the time Greg reached the entrance to the village, a wooden archway at the edge of a field, there were about fifty children following him.

Greg thought he must be approaching Askole. But he'd been through that village before, and nothing here looked familiar. He hoped to see Mouzafer waiting for him at the edge of the village, but instead, standing by the archway, was a wrinkled old man with a gray beard and a hat made of lambswool. His name was Haji Ali, and he was the chief of this village, named Korphe.

"*As-salaam Alaikum* [Peace be with you]," Haji Ali said, shaking Greg's hand. He took Greg through the gate, showed him to an icy river where he could wash his face and hands, and welcomed the stranger into his home.

Haji Ali beat some of the dust from a pile of bedding, put down cushions at the spot of honor close to the hearth, and settled Greg there. Twenty male members of the chief's family came in silently and took their places around the hearth. No one talked as a pot of tea was prepared over a fire of yak dung. Most of the smoke escaped through a square hole in the ceiling. When Greg looked up at the hole, he saw the eyes of the fifty children who had followed him into the village looking down at him. They lay on the roof, peering in at the first foreigner who had ever been to Korphe.

Haji Ali gave Greg a piece of dried meat he had rubbed with leaves of tobacco. Greg didn't like the taste, but he knew it would be rude to refuse. He chewed bravely and choked it down. Then Haji Ali handed him a cup of the *cha*, which he drank with a little more pleasure.

Now that Greg had been welcomed properly, as a guest should be, Haji Ali wanted to know what he was doing in Korphe. He leaned forward, thrust his bearded face in front of Greg's, and demanded, in Balti, to know what had brought this stranger to his village.

With a few words of Balti and a lot of gestures, Greg told the crowd that he was an American, that he'd tried to climb K2, that he had become weak and sick, and that he'd walked here to Askole to find transport that could take him to a bigger city.

"*Cheezaley!* [What the heck!]" Haji Ali said in Balti. "Not Askole," Haji Ali told Greg, laughing. He pointed at the ground by his feet. "Korphe."

Greg was exhausted, but at these words he sat bolt upright, alarmed. He had never heard of Korphe, and never seen it on a map. He explained that he had to get to Askole to meet a man named Mouzafer, who was carrying most of his belongings.

Haji Ali pushed Greg back on the pillows. His son, Twaha, who spoke a little English, translated his father's words. "Today walking Askole no go. Big problem. Half one day's trekking. *Inshallah* [God willing], tomorrow Haji send man find Mouzafer. Now you sleep."

In spite of his worry and his anger at himself for missing the trail again, Greg did lie back on the bed and fell deeply asleep.

13

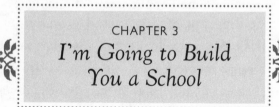

Someone tucked a heavy quilt over Greg. For the first time in months, he slept indoors. When he woke, he was alone, and blue sky showed through the square hole in the ceiling. Haji Ali's wife, Sakina, brought him *lassi*, a drink made with yogurt; a flat bread called *chapatti*; and tea with lots of sugar. Greg wolfed everything down, and Sakina, laughing, brought him more. Greg didn't know at the time how little sugar the Balti had and how precious they considered it. If he had, he would have said no to the second cup of sweet tea.

Sakina left Greg alone, and he looked around the room. Everything from the blackened pots and pans to the oil lanterns looked plain and well used. But not the quilt Greg had slept under. It was made of maroon silk and decorated with tiny mirrors. All the other blankets in the room were thin, worn wool, patched with scraps. Greg realized that his hosts had covered him up with the most valuable thing they owned.

Greg spent the day in Korphe. Late that afternoon, he heard voices calling. He and most of the rest of the village walked to a cliff that overlooked the Braldu River. There he saw someone crossing the river—but not on a bridge. A wooden box hung from a steel cable that had been strung above the water. A person could sit in the box and pull him- or herself along the cable. Crossing the river this way saved the half day of travel needed to walk to the nearest bridge. But it didn't look terribly safe—and a fall would mean certain death.

When the person was halfway across, Greg recognized him—it was Mouzafer, sitting on top of Greg's pack. Once Mouzafer reached the other side, he again slapped Greg on the back, looked him up and down, and shouted, "*Allah Akbhar!*"

After a meal of roasted chicken at Haji Ali's house, Mouzafer and Greg left Korphe. They met up with Scott Darsney, and the two climbers made the long journey by jeep down to the city of Skardu. But Greg felt something tugging him back to Korphe and returned as soon as he could arrange for a ride. He stayed in Haji Ali's house and rested, recovering his strength. Now that he was out of danger, Greg realized just how weakened he had become. He would walk around the village for a few hours each day, with children holding his hands, and then return to Haji Ali's to sleep or simply lie down, staring at the sky.

As Greg slowly got better, he learned more and more about how people lived in this part of Pakistan, called Baltistan. The village of Korphe was perched on a rocky mountain slope, and the people there worked amazingly hard to grow the food they ate—apricots, barley, potatoes—and to take care of the animals they raised. Greg found out that the nearest doctor lived a week's walk away, and that many of the people in Korphe had diseases that would be easily cured in the United States. Most of the children did not get quite enough to eat and suffered from **malnutrition**. One out of three children died before the age of one.

Greg knew he owed the people of Korphe more than he could repay. But he was determined to try. He began giving away the things he had brought with him. Small, useful items like Nalgene water bottles or flashlights were precious to the Balti. He gave Sakina, Haji Ali's wife, his camping stove. He handed Twaha, the chief's son, his fleece jacket, even though it was several sizes too big. To Haji Ali he gave the parka that had kept him warm on K2.

But it turned out that the best thing he had to offer the people of Korphe was his knowledge. In the United States, Greg worked as an emergency room nurse, and he had a medical kit with him. He began to go from house to house, doing what he could to cure injuries and illnesses with simple tools—**antibiotic** ointment to keep wounds from getting infected, **painkillers** to ease suffering. People in and around Korphe began to call him "Dr. Greg," no matter how many times he explained that he was really a nurse.

Greg wanted to do more. While he was spending time with the children of Korphe, he felt like his little sister, Christa, was there, too. "Everything about their life was a struggle," Greg says. "They reminded me of the way Christa . . . had a way of just persevering, no matter what life threw at her." Maybe, he thought, he could get some textbooks or supplies for Korphe's school. He asked Haji Ali if he could see where the children of Korphe went to learn. Haji Ali seemed reluctant, but finally agreed to take Greg there the next morning.

After breakfast, Haji Ali led Greg up a steep path to an open piece of land. Seventy-eight boys and four girls were kneeling on the frosty ground to study. Haji Ali explained that Korphe had no school building. A teacher cost one dollar a day, which was more than the village could afford to pay. They shared a teacher with a nearby village, and he came to Korphe three days a week. The rest of the time the students were left alone to practice the lessons he had left behind.

Greg watched and listened as the children sang Pakistan's national anthem to start their school day. He saw Twaha's seven-year-old daughter, Jahan, standing tall and straight beneath her headscarf as she sang. When the song ended, they sat down in the dirt and began writing out their multiplication tables. A few, like Jahan, had slates on which they wrote with sticks dipped in mud. The rest scratched in the dirt with sticks. "Can you imagine a fourth-grade class in America, alone, without a teacher, sitting there quietly and working on their lessons?" Greg asked later. "I felt like my heart was being torn out. . . . I knew I had to do something."

But what could he do? He had barely enough money left to travel by jeep and bus to Islamabad, Pakistan's capital, where

Greg with children from Korphe

he would catch an airplane to fly home. Still, there had to be something.

Standing next to Haji Ai, looking at the mountains that he'd come halfway around the world to climb, Greg suddenly felt that reaching the summit of K2 to place a necklace there wasn't really important. He could do something much better than that to honor his sister, Christa. He put his hands on Haji Ali's shoulders. "I *will* build a school," he said. "I promise."

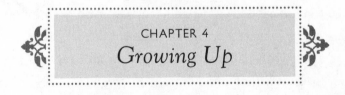

$G$reg Mortenson was born in Minnesota, like his father before him. But in 1958, when he was only three months old, his parents took him along on the great adventure of their lives: working as teachers in a girls' school in the African country of Tanganyika, later renamed Tanzania. It was Greg's father, Irvin, nicknamed Dempsey after a famous boxer, who had the idea. "Dempsey had the travel bug," his wife, Jerene, said. "He loved seeing more of the world. He came home one day while I was pregnant with Greg and said, 'They need teachers in Tanganyika. Let's go to Africa.' I couldn't say no. We just did it."

After four years of working in the Usambara Mountains, the family moved to a city called Moshi, near Mount Kilimanjaro. There, in a cinder-block house with a big pepper tree in the front yard, Greg Mortenson grew up. "The older I get, the more I appreciate my childhood. It was paradise," he said.

Dempsey worked hard to set up the first teaching hospital in Tanzania, a place to help people and train doctors. It was called the **Kilimanjaro Christian Medical Centre**. Jerene worked just as hard to start Moshi International School, where Greg went along with children from countries all over the world. "It was like a little United Nations," Greg said. "There were

The Mortensons in Tanzania, with foster son Mathias Moshi; 1967

twenty-eight different nationalities, and we celebrated all of the holidays: Hanukkah, Christmas, **Diwali**, the **Feast of Id**."

Greg learned to speak **Swahili** perfectly and joined an African dance troupe. At the age of eleven he climbed Mount Kilimanjaro, Africa's highest mountain (19,340 feet). Greg admitted that, after nagging his father to take him, he hated the climb. But once he got to the top, he felt differently. "Standing on the summit at dawn, seeing the sweep of the African **savannah** below me, hooked me on climbing," he remembered.

Greg had three sisters: Kari, Sonja Joy, and Christa, the youngest, born when Greg was twelve. When Christa was baptized, Greg was her godfather.

Christa was small and delicate. As a toddler she had a very bad reaction to a shot of smallpox vaccine, and when she was three she became sick with **meningitis**, a serious illness that can cause headaches, vomiting, and a high fever. Jerene believed that Christa was never the same after the vaccination and the illness. By the time Christa was eight, she began to have **seizures** and was diagnosed with **epilepsy**.

Christa struggled to do simple things that her brother and sisters had learned easily. It took her more than an hour to put on her clothes. She learned to read quickly, but did not understand the meanings of the words on the page—to her, they were just sounds. Greg became her protector, helping her and shielding her from anyone who teased her. "Christa was the nicest of us," he said. "It would take her forever to dress herself in the morning, so she'd lay her clothes out the night before, trying not to take up so much of our time before school. She was remarkably sensitive to other people."

Just after Greg's fourteenth birthday, the hospital his father had worked so hard to create was ready to open. One of the most important things about the hospital, for Dempsey, was making sure that local Tanzanian students would have a chance to train there and become doctors. He didn't want the hospital to be managed by foreigners; he wanted the Tanzanians to run it themselves.

Dempsey threw a huge barbecue to celebrate the opening of the hospital and gave a speech. "I have a prediction to make," he said in Swahili. "In ten years, the head of every department at the Kilimanjaro Christian Medical Center will be a Tanzanian. It's your hospital. It's your country."

"I could feel the swell of pride from the Africans," Greg remembered. "He was saying, 'Look what you've done for yourselves and how much more you can do.' . . . Watching him up there, I felt so proud that this big, barrel-chested man was my father. He taught me, he taught all of us, that if you believe in yourself, you can accomplish anything."

With the hospital and the school finished, the Mortensons decided that it was time to return to the United States. They packed up all their books and weavings and wood carvings and moved back to St. Paul, Minnesota.

The children knew the United States only from brief visits and letters from relatives. But when Greg started high school, he was relieved to see that many of the students were black.

It made him feel that he was not so far away from Moshi. But after word spread around school that the tall new kid was from Africa, a basketball player shoved Greg up against a water fountain and looked him over. "You ain't no African," he sneered, and led his friends in beating up the white boy who could speak Swahili.

Despite the bad start, in most ways Greg was able to settle in. He made good grades and did well as a defensive lineman on the football team. But he did have one habit from his years in Africa that didn't help him fit into life in the United States. "Greg has never been on time in his life," his mother said. "Ever since he was a boy, Greg has always operated on African time." In Africa, many people have a more relaxed attitude toward time than is common in the United States. What an African would consider on time, an American would probably think of as late. Greg never adjusted to the kind of scheduled life that most Americans think of as normal.

The Mortenson family did not have enough money to pay for college, so Greg enlisted in the U.S. Army for two years. After that, the government would provide the money to send him to college under the terms of the **GI Bill**. Four days after his graduation from high school, Greg was in basic training. He was trained as a **medic** and then served in Germany, where he seized the chance to travel around Europe: Rome, London, Amsterdam.

Once his time in the army was over, Greg chose to go to Concordia College, in Minnesota, where he played football.

Two years later, he transferred to the larger University of South Dakota. He washed dishes and worked as an **orderly** in a hospital to make money, sending some of his wages home to his parents each month.

While Greg was studying chemistry and nursing in college, his father became very ill with cancer. Greg offered to drop out of school to take care of his father, but Dempsey told him, "Don't you dare." So Greg made a six-hour drive home to Minnesota every other weekend to spend time with his father, carrying him outside so he could sit in a lawn chair in the sun.

Dempsey died in September 1981, when his son was twenty-three. At the funeral, Greg gave a speech and spoke in Swahili, calling his father "*Baba, kaka, ndugu* [father, brother, friend]."

After losing his father, Greg began to worry about losing Christa, who was having more and more seizures. After he had graduated from the University of South Dakota with a degree in both nursing and chemistry, Greg returned to St. Paul to spend a year with his younger sister. He helped her find a job in a factory, rode buses with her around the city until she felt confident that she could find her way herself, and gave her advice about dating. Christa's needs were also on his mind when he thought about what he wanted to do with his life. He went back to college and chose to study the human body's **nervous system** at Indiana University, hoping that he might come up with something that could help Christa with her seizures. But the kind of medical research needed to cure diseases like epilepsy moves slowly—too slowly for Greg. He began to feel that what he needed was a different kind of life, one where he could spend his time outdoors, not cooped up in classrooms and labs. He wanted to climb mountains.

With just a few thousand dollars in his savings account, Greg packed up his car and headed out to California. He got a job as an emergency room nurse, and, when he wasn't at the hospital, he was working out in a climbing gym, running marathons, reading books about famous climbers, or hiking and climbing on a mountain.

On July 24, 1992, when Greg was thirty-four, he fell nearly eight hundred vertical feet while climbing a mountain. He was lucky; he had only put his shoulder out of joint and broken a bone in his arm. When he got to an emergency room and called his mother to let her know he would be all right, she had terrible news. Christa and her mom had planned to go to the Field of Dreams in Dyersville, Iowa, for Christa's twenty-third birthday. *Field of Dreams* was her favorite movie, and she had wanted to see the place where it was filmed. But at the same time that Greg was falling down the mountain, his mother went to wake Christa for their trip, and found that she'd died of a seizure.

After Christa's death, Greg wasn't sure what to do with himself. A call from a fellow mountain climber, Dan Mazur, helped him decide. Mazur was putting together an expedition to K2. He asked Greg to come. Greg knew this was the way he wanted to honor his sister's memory—by making it to the peak of K2 in her honor.

❦ ❦ ❦

But Greg hadn't reached the summit of K2. And now in the fall of 1993, back home from Pakistan, Greg had a new challenge ahead of him. He packed his climbing gear away in a rented storage space and tried to figure out how he was going to accomplish his new goal: raising enough money to build a school in Korphe. How could he convince Americans to care about a circle of children sitting in the cold on the other side of the world, scratching their lessons in the dirt with sticks? This might be even harder than climbing the second-highest mountain on Earth.

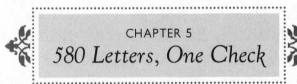

## CHAPTER 5
### 580 Letters, One Check

Greg knew how to climb a mountain. He knew how to handle a badly hurt patient in the emergency room. But he didn't really know how to raise money for a school. He couldn't even use a computer, so he rented a typewriter and slowly tapped out letters to anyone he could think of who had money and might want to help. He wrote to sports heroes like Michael Jordan, talk-show hosts like Oprah Winfrey, **news anchors**, politicians, and movie stars like Susan Sarandon. Time after time he made mistakes on the typewriter. His hands felt almost too big for the keyboard. So he would yank the paper out of the typewriter, crumple it up, and start over.

Things started moving a little faster when Greg went to the store where he usually rented a typewriter and found it closed. He tried another store down the block. The owner told him, "This is 1993, why don't you rent a computer?" When Greg explained that he didn't know how to use one and told the man what he needed the typewriter for, the man decided to help. His name was Kishwar Syed, and he was from Pakistan. "My village in Pakistan had no school, so the importance of what Greg was trying to do was very dear to me," he said. "His cause was so great that it was my duty to devote myself to help him." He sat Greg down in front of a computer and gave him lessons in how to use it. Greg realized that the letters he had been pecking out so slowly on the typewriter could now be done in one day. With Syed's help he sent out 580 letters.

While he was waiting for a response from his letters, Greg heard from his mother. She was now the principal of Westside Elementary School in River Falls, Wisconsin, and she asked her son to come to the school and talk to the students about the children of Korphe and what he was trying to do for them. "It was hard to explain to adults why I wanted to help students in Pakistan," Greg said. "But the kids got it right away. When they saw the pictures, they couldn't believe that there was a place where children sat outside in cold weather and tried to hold classes without teachers. They decided to do something about it."

The students started a "Pennies for Pakistan" drive and collected 62,345 pennies. They sent Greg a check for $623.45. "Children took the first step to build the school," he said. "And they did it with something that's basically worthless in our society—pennies. But . . . pennies can move mountains." Maybe now, Greg thought, his luck would change.

But Greg's luck wasn't changing as much as he'd hoped.

Apart from the check from the students at his mother's school, he got only one other donation in response to his 580 letters. Tom Brokaw, a television news anchor who, like Greg, had attended the University of South Dakota, sent a check for one hundred dollars. Greg was far short of the twelve thousand dollars he'd figured he'd need to build the school.

Greg was living as cheaply as possible, saving all his money for the school and the trip he hoped to make back to Korphe. Instead of renting an apartment, he kept everything he owned in a small storage space. He slept in his car, wrapped in the sleeping bag that had kept him warm on K2. And he kept thinking of what he could do to make the school happen. When he talked about his project to a friend, Dr. Tom Vaughan, at the hospital where he worked, Vaughan had an idea. He was also a mountain climber, and he wrote an article about Greg's attempt to climb K2 and his efforts to help the children of Korphe. He published the article in a newsletter put out by the **American Himalayan Foundation** (AHF), a **nonprofit** group that works to help the people of the Himalayas. Many readers of the newsletter were mountain climbers. Maybe they would be interested in another climber's project to help the children of Pakistan.

It turned out that one of them was.

🐦 🐦 🐦

Jean Hoerni was a mountain climber and a scientist who had created a new kind of process to store information on computer chips. He was brilliant, he was hard to get along with, and by now he had become very rich. He had read Tom Vaughan's article in the newsletter and, through Vaughan, contacted Greg. Greg called him back.

"So. What, exactly, will your school cost?" Hoerni barked at Greg over the phone.

"I met with an architect and a contractor in Skardu, and priced out all the materials," Greg said. "I want it to have five rooms, four for classes and one common room for—"

"A number!" Hoerni snapped.

"Twelve thousand dollars," Greg said nervously, "but whatever you'd like to contribute toward—"

"Is that all?" Hoerni demanded. "You can really build your school for twelve grand?"

A week later a check for twelve thousand dollars arrived in Greg's post office box. With it was a single note, scribbled on a sheet of graph paper. It said, "Don't screw up. Regards, J.H."

Greg had the money for his school.

But he still needed more money to get himself to Pakistan. He sold his books on climbing and some other old, rare books that had belonged to his father. He sold his climbing gear. And finally he sold his car. Having sold nearly everything he owned, he then set off toward the taxi waiting to take him to the airport, where he would catch a flight to Pakistan.

## CHAPTER 6
### Hard Way Home

In the city of Rawalpindi, Greg got the cheapest room possible at the same hotel in which he had stayed when preparing to climb K2. Before heading off to Korphe, he'd need to get everything necessary to build a school.

Abdul Shah, a watchman at the hotel, remembered Greg from his last visit and greeted him when he woke up on his first day. "Mr. Greg, **Sahib**," he inquired, "may I ask why you are coming back?"

"I've come to build a school, *Inshallah*," Greg answered. He told Abdul the story of his attempt to climb K2 and what the people of Korphe had done for him.

Abdul looked doubtfully at Greg, who was wearing worn-out tennis shoes and a shabby, dirty **shalwar kamiz**, the long shirt and baggy pants that are traditional clothes in Pakistan. "You are the rich man?" he asked.

"No," Greg said. He explained that many people in America,

even children, had given what money they could afford to build the school. He showed Abdul the green nylon sack, stuffed with hundred-dollar bills, that he carried beneath his clothes. "This is exactly enough for one school, if I'm very careful," he said.

Abdul got to his feet. "By the merciful light of Allah Almighty, tomorrow we make much bargain. We must bargain very well," he said.

❦ ❦ ❦

Over the next few days, Abdul helped Greg buy everything he needed: lumber, cement, nails, hammers, saws, axes, shovels, sheets of tin for the roof. When owners of stores asked for high prices, Abdul argued with them, told them that the supplies were for a school being built as an act of charity, and bargained them down to what Greg could afford. It sometimes took hours of conversation, over many cups of tea. He even brought Greg to a tailor to get two new sets of *shalwar kamiz* when the old shirt he was wearing ripped from collar to hem. The tailor took Greg in hand as well. When Greg asked about **Islam**, he taught him to pray in the traditional way, facing Mecca, where the body of the prophet, Mohammed, rests.

Finally, with Abdul's help, Greg had what he needed. He was ready for his three-day trip to Korphe.

❦ ❦ ❦

Before dawn the next morning, Abdul woke Greg and handed him his tennis shoes. He'd spent hours while Greg slept scrubbing, mending, and polishing the worn sneakers so that

Ahmed says evening prayers

Greg could look his best. Together, they went to the bazaar where all the supplies Greg had bought would be packed onto a truck, ready to drive to Korphe. It took all day to get everything loaded. A crowd gathered to see this astonishing sight—a tall foreign man in a new *shalwar kamiz* that was already dirty and dusty, collecting supplies for a school for Pakistani children.

Greg watched every item be loaded onto the truck, checking them against a list. Two of the most important items—a level and a plumb line, which would be needed to make sure the walls were straight and the floors were level—were missing. Abdul helped Greg hunt for them, and once the tools were found at the bottom of the load, he wrapped them carefully in a cloth and gave them to the driver, with orders to keep them safe.

Finally, all forty-two lines on the list had been marked off.

Greg said good-bye to Abdul. His new friend said a prayer for his safe journey, and Greg climbed onto the truck and waved good-bye. "*Allah Akbhar!*" the crowd shouted as the truck drove off for Korphe, and Greg continued to wave good-bye.

Greg perched on top of his load of school supplies for much of the drive out of Rawalpindi and into the mountains. Making himself comfortable on a nest of burlap and bags of hay, he settled down with a crate of chickens for company. After a week of haggling over prices and fretting over every penny, he felt like he could finally relax. "It was cool and windy on top of that truck," he remembered. "And I hadn't been cool since I arrived in Rawalpindi. I felt like a king, riding high on my throne. I felt like I'd already succeeded. I'd bought everything we needed and stuck to my budget. . . . And in a few weeks, I thought, the school would be built, and I could head home and figure out what to do with the rest of my life. I don't know if I've ever felt so satisfied."

As the road began to rise into the mountains, it got steadily colder. Greg wrapped a wool blanket around his shoulders and head. Sometimes the wheels spun only a foot away from a deadly drop into a deep gorge. Greg could look down from his perch and see just how close the tires were from the edge of the road. At other times the road was so steep that the driver's assistants had to leap out and wedge rocks behind the truck's wheels to keep it from slipping backward. Then the truck would struggle forward a few feet, and they would snatch up the rocks and shove them beneath the wheels again, inching their way up the slope.

After three days of hair-raising travel, with Greg riding on the top of the load most of the way, they were drawing close to the city of Skardu. From there, Greg would need to hire jeeps to carry the supplies the rest of the way to Korphe. He was getting so close to finishing the school. His happy ending, he felt sure, was just about to begin.

That was right before a branch of a poplar tree smacked him in the face. Another one tore the blanket off his head. Greg had to throw himself facedown on top of his supplies as the truck rolled down a tree-lined street and into Skardu.

Greg told the truck driver to take the truck's contents to the office of Mohammed Ali Changazi. Changazi made a living organizing tours and mountain-climbing expeditions, getting people the supplies and workers they needed. He had helped with Greg's expedition to K2. Afterward Greg had told him about his plans to build a school. Changazi, thought Greg, would know how to get his supplies to Korphe.

Changazi, dressed in a dazzling white *shalwar*, opened the door himself and greeted Greg with a hug. "Dr. Greg," he said. "What are you doing here? Trekking season is over."

"I brought the school!" Greg said. He expected Changazi to be pleased, but the man seemed baffled.

"It's too late to build anything now. And why didn't you buy supplies in Skardu?" he asked. Still, he agreed to let Greg unload the truck and store the supplies in his courtyard. Then they could have tea and discuss the school. He looked at Greg's greasy *shalwar* and at his grimy face and matted hair, filthy from

35

riding for three days on top of the truck. "But why don't you have a wash first, and such like that," he suggested.

Greg cleaned up and slept in Changazi's office. The next morning, he was eager to start for Korphe. But first he ran into a visitor—Akhmalu, the man who had cooked for his K2 expedition. The man reminded Greg of a promise he'd made to visit Akhmalu's village, Khane. "I have one jeep waiting to go to Khane village," he said. "We go now."

"Maybe tomorrow, or the next day," Greg said, looking around for his school supplies in the courtyard outside. He didn't see them.

"But my whole village will expect you, sir," said Akhmalu. "We have prepare special dinner already."

Greg knew that the Balti people did not have much food to spare, and he couldn't bear the idea of making them waste a special meal. He agreed to go. Changazi came along as well, though he didn't seem happy about it.

In Khane, Greg was welcomed into the home of another old acquaintance, Janjungpa, a porter from his expedition to K2. As Greg settled down to a meal of fried chicken, turnip salad, and sheep liver and brains, this man began to speak. "I wish to thank Mr. Girek Mortenson for honoring us and coming to build a school for Khane village," he said.

"A school for Khane?" Greg croaked, almost choking on a bite of chicken.

An argument broke out among the people of Khane about whether Greg had promised to build a school for the children of

Khane or a school for the Balti porters where they could learn better techniques of mountain climbing. Greg protested over and over that he hadn't promised to do either of these things, but nobody was listening.

Eventually, Akhmalu led Greg to his own home, where Greg stayed the night. The next morning Greg insisted that Changazi get him back to Skardu before the arguments could begin all over again. Changazi agreed, and promised to take Greg to the place where the supplies for the school were stored. But, instead, Greg found himself a guest in Changazi's home village, Kuardu. Once again, there was a huge feast spread for him: chicken, radishes and turnips, a rice dish with nuts and raisins, a yak stew. Greg had never seen so much food in one place in Baltistan.

"What are we doing here, Changazi?" he asked. "Where are my supplies?"

"These are the elders of my village," Changazi said, gesturing to several men who had joined them for the meal. "Here in Kuardu, I can promise you no arguments. They have already agreed to see that your school is built in our village before winter."

Greg was so angry that he got up, stepped over the food arranged on the floor, even though he knew how rude this would seem, and hurried out of the room. Outside, he ran up a steep shepherd's path until he reached a little clearing, and there he collapsed and cried as he hadn't cried since Christa's death.

How could he get a school built if he couldn't even get his supplies out of Skardu? Worse yet, he was starting to have doubts about the people of Korphe. Could they really be as good, as kind, as generous as he remembered them? Had he just been so happy to get down alive from K2 that everything in Korphe had seemed wonderful? Maybe all the people there were like Changazi and the other men who were trying to get his school for their own villages—dishonest, greedy, always arguing.

When Greg finally stopped crying, he looked up to see several children. They had brought a herd of goats to graze, but now they were watching the sobbing foreigner. He got up, brushed off his clothes, walked over to them, and knelt down by the oldest, a boy of about eleven.

"What . . . are . . . you?" the boy said shyly, in English, reaching out to shake the stranger's hand.

"I am Greg. I am good," Greg answered, grasping the boy's small hand in his large one.

"I am Greg. I am good," all of the children repeated.

"No, I am Greg. What is your name?" he tried again.

"No, I am Greg. What is your name?" the children echoed, giggling.

Greg switched to Balti, telling them that his name was Greg and that he came from America. He asked what their names were. They clapped, thrilled to understand him, and they each shook his hand as they told him their names. The girls wrapped their hands cautiously in their headscarves before touching the strange American. Greg taught them the word for foreigner, **Angrezi**. He taught them English words for nose, hair, ears, eyes, mouth. Half an hour later, when Changazi found him, Greg was kneeling, drawing multiplication tables in the dirt with a stick for the children to copy.

"Dr. Greg. Come down. Come inside. Have some tea. We have much to discuss," Changazi pleaded.

"We have nothing to discuss until you take me to Korphe," Greg said.

"Korphe is very far. And very dirty. You like these children. Why don't you build your school right here?" Changazi asked.

"No," said Greg. He rubbed out the numbers a nine-year-old girl had written in the dirt and corrected them. "Six times six is thirty-six."

"Greg, Sahib, please."

"Korphe," Mortenson said. "I have nothing to say to you until then."

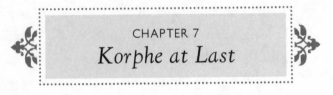

## CHAPTER 7
### Korphe at Last

During the eight-hour drive to Korphe, Greg had plenty of time to think. Maybe he'd been too harsh, too angry, with Changazi and the other men who'd tried to scheme and plot to get the school he'd been planning to build for Korphe. Greg was a man without a house to live in, without a car to drive, and with hardly any money in the bank—but maybe, in Baltistan, a poor section of a poor country, anyone from the United States seemed so rich that people imagined he could give them everything. If the people of Korphe started to argue or fight over what he could do for them, or tried to get him to help some of the villagers and not others, Greg would be more patient, he decided. He would listen to everyone, eat as many meals as necessary, before insisting that the school would have to help every child in Korphe.

It had been dark for hours by the time they arrived at the Braldu River. On the other side of the deep gorge was Korphe

The driver of the jeep honked and flashed his lights. Greg heard a shout from across the water. The jeep turned so that its headlights lit up a small figure pulling himself across the gorge in the rickety wooden box hanging from the steel cable.

Greg recognized Haji Ali's son, Twaha, before the man jumped out of the box and crashed into him. Twaha wrapped his arms around Greg's waist and hugged him tightly. He smelled of smoke and sweat. When he finally loosened his grip, Twaha looked up at the tall American, laughing. "Father mine, Haji Ali, say Allah send you back someday," he said. "Haji Ali know everything, sir."

Twaha helped Greg climb into the cable car to cross the river again. "It was just a box, really," Greg remembered later. "Like a big fruit crate held together with a few nails. You pulled yourself along this greasy cable and tried not to think about the creaking sounds it made. Tried not to think about the obvious—if it broke, you'd fall. And if you fell, you were dead."

Greg pulled himself along 350 feet of cable. The box swayed back and forth in the wind. He could feel spray in the air. A hundred feet below he could feel, but not see, the rushing water of the Braldu scouring boulders smooth. Then, on a bluff high over the riverbank, lit up by the jeep's headlights, he caught sight of hundreds of people waiting to greet him. It looked like everyone in Korphe was waiting for him. On the far right was an unmistakable figure. Standing like he was carved out of rock, his legs planted wide, Haji Ali watched Greg make his slow way across the river.

Haji Ali's granddaughter, Jahan, remembers that evening

Haji Ali, Korphe village chief and Greg's mentor

well. "Many climbers make promises to the Balti people and forget them when they find their way home," she said. "My grandfather told us many times that Dr. Greg was different. He would come back. But we were surprised to see him again so soon. And I was so surprised to see, once again, his long body. None of the Braldu people look like that. He was very . . . surprising."

Haji Ali praised Allah for bringing Greg back, and then hugged him tightly. Later, by a roaring fire in Haji Ali's house, Greg felt completely at home. He sat happily, surrounded by the people he'd been thinking about all these months. He was bursting to tell Haji Ali that he had kept his promise, but first he had to be polite and wait to be served tea.

Sakina, Haji Ali's wife, brought out an old package of sugar

42

cookies and gave them to Greg on a chipped tray with a cup of butter tea. He broke the cookies into tiny pieces, took one, and passed the tray around so that everyone could share. Haji Ali waited until Greg had sipped his tea. Then he slapped him on his knee, grinning. Once again, he asked what this foreigner was doing in Korphe. But this time Greg hadn't wandered into Korphe because he'd lost his way. He'd come with good news, and he ached to deliver it.

"I bought everything we need to build a school," he said in Balti. He had rehearsed the words so that he'd get them right. "All the wood, and cement and tools. It's all in Skardu right now. I came back to keep my promise." He looked Haji Ali in the eye. "And I hope we can begin building it soon, *Inshallah*."

"Dr. Greg," Haji Ali said in Balti. "By the most merciful blessings of Allah you have come back to Korphe. I believed you would and said so as often as the wind blew through the Braldu Valley. That's why we have all discussed the school while you were in America. We want very much a school for Korphe." Haji Ali fastened his eyes on Greg's. "But we have decided. . . . Before it is possible to build a school, we must build a bridge. This is what Korphe needs now."

Greg hoped that he had misunderstood. Maybe there was a problem with his Balti. "A bridge?" he said in English.

"Yes, the big bridge, the stone one," Twaha said, also in English. "So we can carry the school to Korphe village."

Greg took a long sip of tea. He took another. He was thinking hard.

Sitting by the fire in Haji Ali's home, Greg's mind raced. He'd worked so hard and given up so much to get to this moment— and now he was being told that he couldn't build his school in Korphe after all. But then his thoughts slowed and settled until he felt surprisingly calm.

He was disappointed, but not angry. Haji Ali was right. Of course Korphe needed a bridge. How had Greg been planning to build his school? Had he thought he'd carry every piece of plywood and every sheet of tin in a rickety wooden cable car above the dangerous Braldu River? It was himself he was angry with. He should have planned better. He decided to stay in Korphe until he understood everything he had to do to make the school possible.

"Tell me about this bridge," he asked Haji Ali. "What do we need? How do we get started?"

He hoped that the bridge might be built simply and cheaply. That hope didn't last long.

"We have to blast many dynamite and cut many stone," Twaha began. That started off an argument among the men of the village about where to get the stone—cut it from the mountains nearby, or have it brought in by jeep? But there was no argument about what else they'd need. Steel cable and planks of wood would have to be bought and transported to Korphe. It would all cost thousands of dollars. Thousands of dollars that Greg didn't have.

Greg told everyone that he'd spent his money already, buying supplies for the school, and that he'd have to return to America and raise more. He expected them to be as disappointed as he felt. But the Balti people were used to waiting. They spent half the year huddled inside, breathing the smoke from yak dung fires, waiting for the winter to pass so they could go outside again. A Balti hunter might track a mountain goat for days before he was close enough to risk shooting the only bullet he could afford. The people of Korphe had gotten very good at being patient. They didn't seem worried at all.

"Thanyouvermuch," Haji Ali said, trying to speak English. Greg was almost ashamed to be thanked for a school he hadn't brought them because he hadn't planned well enough. He hugged the old man tight against his chest. Haji Ali beamed and told Sakina to pour Greg a fresh cup of butter tea. Greg was beginning to like the stuff more each time he tasted it.

Later, Greg and Haji Ali rode along the river in a jeep, studying how bridges were constructed. Greg drew a sketch in his notebook of the kind of bridge the people of Korphe wanted.

And he met with the village elders to discuss which piece of land he should build his school on when, *Inshallah*, he returned from America.

In December, nearly two months after he'd arrived, as snow was blanketing Korphe, Greg said his good-byes. After visiting half the houses in Korphe for a farewell cup of tea, he bounced in a jeep back toward Skardu and the long journey home to America.

🐛 🐛 🐛

Greg came back to San Francisco and began a hard time in his life. He'd been gone months longer than he'd expected. He had eighty-three dollars in the bank. His girlfriend had started seeing someone else. And his boss at the hospital told him he no longer had a job. "You're one of the best we have, Greg, but if you don't show up, you're useless to me. You're fired," he said. Even after Greg had found a new job and scraped together enough money to rent a room, things didn't get much better.

Lonely, mostly broke, and nearly hopeless, he felt as if he'd failed the people of Korphe. How could he get them the money for the bridge? He didn't have the courage to call Jean Hoerni, who had sent the money for the school, to ask for more. He didn't know what to do until a phone call gave him a new direction.

The call was from Dr. Louis Reichardt, the first American to reach the summit of K2. Before his own attempt to climb that mountain, Greg had called Reichardt to ask for his advice. The two of them had talked from time to time since then, and

Reichardt knew Jean Hoerni. Now he'd called to ask Greg how he was. "Jean told me what you're trying to do with your school," Reichardt said. "How's it going?"

Greg told him the whole story, from the 580 letters to the bridge that needed to be built, from losing his girlfriend to losing his job.

"Pull yourself together, Greg," Reichardt said. "Of course you've hit a few speed bumps. But what you're trying to do is much more difficult than climbing K2."

"Coming from Lou Reichardt, those words meant a lot," Greg said later. "He was one of my heroes." Reichardt had very nearly died in his attempt to reach the summit of K2. He knew about doing everything you could to reach a goal that was almost impossible. Hearing this man tell him that what he was trying to do was tough, but not out of his reach, made Greg think that maybe he hadn't failed. Not yet.

"Call Jean and tell him everything you've told me," Reichardt said. "Ask him to pay for the bridge. Believe me, he can afford it."

For the first time since he'd gotten home, Greg began to feel like himself. He dug through his papers for Jean Hoerni's phone number. Hoerni had told him not to screw up. Well, maybe he had. Maybe he hadn't. It depended on who you talked to. He dialed the number. And then the phone was ringing.

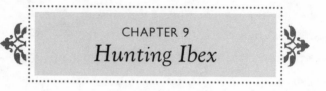

Talking to Jean Hoerni had not been as frightening as Greg had expected. The millionaire had been surprisingly kind, agreeing to send a check for another ten thousand dollars. He asked for only one thing. "Get the school built as quickly as you can. And when you finish, bring me a photo," he demanded. "I'm not getting any younger." Greg promised that he would.

By June 1995, Greg was back in Pakistan. In Skardu, he bargained for all the supplies he needed to build a bridge. Finally, after a dozen tries, he found someone who would sell him five spools of steel cable—the last item on his list. "And may I know what you want with so much cable?" the seller asked.

"My friends' village in the upper Braldu Valley has no bridge. I'm going to help them build one," Greg explained.

"Ah, you are American, yes?"

"Yes, sir."

"I've heard about your bridge," the seller remarked. He asked if the roads to Korphe could be traveled by jeep.

"If it doesn't start raining," Greg replied. "Can you deliver the cable?"

"*Inshallah.*"

Allah willing. It was a good answer. Now that he had everything he needed, Greg hoped the bridge could be finished before the winter. Then, next spring, work on the school could start.

Greg took a jeep from Skardu to the town of Askole. As he traveled, it started to rain, and the rain turned into a downpour. A monsoon had swept in. The jeep driver refused to continue on the muddy road from Askole to Korphe, so Greg set off on foot. The men of Korphe met him, hours later, and took him over to the village in the hanging basket. On either side of the river, slabs of granite were stacked high. They had been cut from the local hillsides and would be used to create the two towers between which the bridge would be built.

At Haji Ali's house, his wife, Sakina, took Greg's hand in welcome. He realized that it was the first time a Balti woman had touched him. It is against tradition for a woman among the Balti to touch a man who isn't related to her, even to shake hands. The moment meant that, to Sakina, Greg was becoming like family.

Sakina grinned boldly up at Greg, as if daring him to be surprised. In response, he did something that surprised her—he stepped into her kitchen, a small area of the house with a ring of rocks to hold a fire, a few shelves, and a wooden board on the floor for chopping. Normally only the women in the house would do any work in the kitchen.

Greg said hello to Sakina's granddaughter, Jahan, who giggled and tugged her headscarf over her face. As Sakina, laughing, tried to shoo him out of her kitchen, Greg filled a pot with tea leaves and water, added a few sticks of kindling to the fire, and put the tea on to boil.

"My grandmother was very shocked when Dr. Greg went into her kitchen," Jahan said later. "But she already thought of him as her own child, so she accepted it. Soon, her ideas changed, and she began to tease my grandfather that he should learn to be more helpful like his American son."

Greg poured the tea and served it to Haji Ali and the other elders of Korphe while Haji Ali told them how things were going with the bridge. "I was always amazed at how, without a telephone, electricity, or a radio, Haji Ali kept himself informed of everything that was happening in the Braldu Valley and beyond," Greg said. Now he told Greg and the other men gathered in his house that two jeeps carrying the cable for the bridge had been stopped by a rockslide about eighteen miles away from Korphe. The road might stay blocked for weeks, especially in such bad weather. So Haji Ali suggested that every man in the village pitch in and carry the cable to Korphe so that work on the bridge could begin at once.

The next morning a group of men, from teenagers to old men, set out. Greg was surprised at their cheerfulness as they walked all day in the rain to reach the stranded jeeps and then turned around again to walk twelve hours back to Korphe, this time carrying spools of cable that each weighed eight hundred pounds and took ten men to lift.

The men chewed tobacco and seemed happy as they marched. Working this hard to improve life in their village, rather than to help foreigners climb mountains, was a pleasure, Haji Ali's son, Twaha, told Greg as he walked.

After they'd carried the cable to the waterside, the men dug the foundations for the bridge. But the rain continued. They couldn't pour concrete for the bridge in the rain; it wouldn't harden in the wet weather. So Twaha and some of the men invited Greg on an ibex hunt while they waited for the weather to clear.

Ibex are large, muscular mountain goats with remarkable curling horns. The Balti prize the horns as much as they love the animal's meat. Sure-footed and strong, ibex can graze higher on mountain slopes than their predators—wolves and snow leopards—can travel.

Greg, Twaha, and the others walked out of Korphe in a steady rain, Twaha carrying a gun over his shoulder. To Greg, the gun looked like it belonged in a museum; he couldn't believe they were really going to shoot anything with it. As they walked, Greg saw the bridge he had missed on his way down from K2, the one that led toward Askole. He felt cheerful, thinking how much less interesting his life would have been if he hadn't taken the wrong turn and ended up in Korphe, which now felt like his second home.

An ibex

Just as they reached the foot of a glacier, the rain finally stopped. Twaha reached into a pocket and took out a small, round medallion woven of colorful wool. A **tomar**, or a badge of courage, it was meant to keep away evil spirits. Every baby born into a Balti tribe is given one at birth. No Balti would think of doing something as dangerous as crossing a glacier without a **tomar**. Now Twaha carefully tied the little medallion to the zipper of Greg's jacket, to keep him safe on the ice.

The men picked a path through shifting slabs of ice and around deep blue pools. Water echoed from inside deep cracks in the glacier's surface, and the sound of rocks falling down the ice shattered the silence. Twaha pointed out the tracks of a snow leopard, and two vultures circled overhead. Greg's feet, in his Nikes, were soon freezing. But one of the hunters, Hussein, took handfuls of hay out of his pack and stuffed them inside Greg's shoes. That made the cold bearable—just.

It took them four days to spot their first ibex. It was dead, picked clean by vultures, perhaps killed by an **avalanche**. But high on a ledge above the bones, a herd of sixteen ibex were grazing.

Twaha tied the bleached skull and curving horns of the dead ibex to Greg's backpack, as a present. Then they hiked up to the high ridge where the ibex were grazing. Twice they tried to circle around to find a spot where the wind would not blow their scent to the goats. But each time the herd sensed them and bounded away before they were close enough to try a shot.

Just before dusk on the seventh day, Twaha spotted a big male ibex on an outcropping sixty feet above them. He tipped gunpowder and a bullet into his gun, while Greg and the others pressed themselves against the base of a cliff, hoping to stay hidden. Greg saw Twaha's mouth moving in prayer as he pulled the trigger. The sound of the gun was deafening, and it brought a rain of pebbles dancing down from the heights. At first Greg thought that Twaha had missed. Then the ibex's front legs buckled, and it pitched over onto its side. "*Allah-u-Akbhar!*" the men all shouted.

They butchered the ibex in a cave, by firelight, cutting up the meat and preparing it to be carried back to the village. Hussein, who had lined Greg's shoes with straw, wielded a long, curved knife like an expert. He was the only one of Korphe's men who had been educated; he'd left the village to go all the way through twelfth grade in a city far from the mountains. Hussein, Greg realized, would be a perfect teacher for the school once it was built. He knew all about life in Korphe, but he also knew what the children there would need to learn.

By the time the hunters arrived back in Korphe, the rains had ended and the weather was crisp and clear. Twaha marched in front, holding up the head of the ibex like a trophy. Greg brought up the rear. They handed out little cubes of ibex fat to the children, who sucked on them like candy. The meat, several hundred pounds of it, was shared out among the hunters' families.

## CHAPTER 10
## *Building Bridges*

The weather was now clear enough for work on the bridge to begin. First two stone towers, each sixty-four feet high, had to be built, one on each side of the river. Four men lifted each block of stone, straining to place it straight and level on top of the cement that would hold it in place. The women took care of the crops in the fields as the men worked on the bridge. Children watched as their fathers and uncles lifted the heavy slabs and shouted encouragement. Block by block, the towers rose.

During the warm summer months, the people of Korphe lived outdoors as much as they could. Their two meals a day were usually eaten on the flat roofs of their houses. After a long, satisfying day of working on the bridge, Greg loved washing down a bowl of rice and lentil stew with strong tea, basking in the sun with Haji Ali's family, and chatting across the rooftops to the other families doing the same thing. On the warm, dry roof, eating, smoking, and gossiping, Greg felt sure that, although there were many things the Balti did not have, they did have an uncomplicated happiness that was becoming very rare in the world.

At night, unmarried men like Greg and Twaha often slept on the rooftops, under the stars. The two had long talks. Twaha confessed how much he missed his wife, who had died giving birth to their daughter, Jahan. "Will you marry again?" Greg asked.

"Oh, for me this is very easy," Twaha explained. "One day I will be **nurmadhar** [chief] and already I have lots of land. So far I don't love any other woman." He was curious about his friend's love life as well. "You have a sweetheart in your village?" he asked.

Greg talked about the women he had dated, including the one who had broken up with him the last time he was in Pakistan.

"Ah, she left you because you had no house," said Twaha. "This thing happens often in Baltistan. But now you can tell her you have a house and almost a bridge in Korphe."

"She's not the one I want," said Greg.

"Then you better quickly find your woman," Twaha said, "before you grow too old and fat."

🌱 🌱 🌱

The day the men strung the first cable between the two towers, Greg delivered a letter. He was watching as the workers stretched the cable tightly with teams of yaks and fastened it to the towers. But he also had an eye out for a party of Americans that he had heard would be coming down the trail from the Baltoro Glacier.

Then he saw the person he was looking for—a man in a white baseball cap, leaning on a walking stick, with a big, muscular guide at his side. His name was George McCown, and he was the **board** director of the American Himalayan Foundation. It was the AHF's newsletter that had first published the article about Greg and his school for Korphe, which led Jean Hoerni to donate the funds for the school. McCown had spent his sixtieth birthday hiking to K2, and the AHF had sent him a birthday card. Not sure how to get it to him, the authorities in Askole had handed it to Greg. They had figured one American would be able to find another.

Grinning, Greg now walked over to the other American. "Are you George McCown?" he asked. McCown nodded, amazed, and Greg handed him the card. "Then happy birthday," he said, grinning.

Greg told McCown how the money for Korphe's school had been raised after the AHF's newsletter had printed an article about his project. "Greg's a guy you immediately like and trust," said McCown. "Watching all those people work with him to build that bridge, it was obvious they loved him. He operated as one of them."

Greg asked McCown to do him a favor. "I was feeling out on a limb in Korphe, operating all by myself," Greg explained later. "And I wanted these people to feel like it wasn't just me, that there were a bunch of other Americans back home concerned about helping them." He gave McCown a roll of **rupees** and asked him to pay everybody the money they were owed for their work on the bridge, as if he were "the big boss from America."

"So I hammed it up," McCown said. "I walked around like a chief, paying everyone their wages, telling them they were doing a great job, and to really throw themselves into it, and finish as fast as they could."

Greg introduced himself to McCown's guide as well. When he tried to talk to the man in Balti, the guide answered in a different language—**Urdu**. Greg learned he was from the **Wakhi** tribe, near the Afghanistan border, and his name was Faisal Baig.

McCown and Baig made their way back toward Askole, but they didn't walk out of Greg's life. Later, Baig would volunteer to serve as Greg's personal bodyguard, and McCown would become an important supporter of Greg's work.

🐝 🐝 🐝

In late August 1995, ten weeks after they had started, the work on the bridge was at last complete. Haji Ali offered Greg the last piece of wood and asked him to lay it in place. But Greg insisted that Korphe's chief complete Korphe's bridge. Haji Ali raised the plank high over his head and thanked Allah for the foreigner he'd been kind enough to send to this village. Then he knelt and laid the board in place. The women and children of Korphe shouted their approval.

Then Greg prepared to head back to California, where he

would spend the winter and spring earning enough money to return to start building the school at last. He spent his last night in Korphe with Haji Ali, Twaha, and Hussein. Hussein had offered to donate a field that his wife, Hawa, owned. The school could be built there. It had a clear view of the mountain called Korphe K2, which Greg thought would encourage students to aim high. Greg agreed, if Hussein would promise to become the school's first teacher. They settled the deal over sweet tea and handshakes, and talked until long after dark.

Below them, lantern lights flickered over the Braldu River as the people of Korphe walked back and forth across their new bridge. For the first time they were really connected to the outside world, the world to which Greg was getting ready to return.

Before Greg left, he did one more thing. He dug tent pegs into the frozen soil of the field Hussein had given for the school, and tied red and blue nylon cord to them, marking out a plan for five rooms. He also left Haji Ali enough money to hire workers from nearby villages to cut stone and carry it to Korphe. They should be able to lay a foundation, or base, for the school before Greg came back.

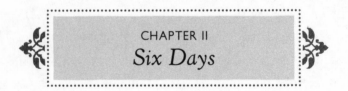

Back in the United States, Greg visited Jean Hoerni in Seattle and brought him pictures of the bridge, as promised. "I was afraid of Jean, at first," he admitted. "But he couldn't have been kinder to me." Greg unpacked his duffel bag, and soon he and Hoerni were bent over a coffee table, studying photos, architectural drawings, and maps.

Hoerni had trekked to K2 base camp twice, and he and Greg talked about all of the villages that, like Korphe, didn't appear on maps. Hoerni was very pleased to be able to draw in black marker the new bridge over the Braldu River on a map.

"Jean really responded to Greg right away," Hoerni's wife, Jennifer Wilson, remembered later. "He appreciated how goofy and unbusinesslike Greg was. . . . Jean had accomplished a lot in his life. But the challenge of building the Korphe School excited him just as much as his scientific work. He really felt a connection to the region. After Greg left, he told me, 'I think this young guy has a fifty-fifty chance of getting the job done. And if he does, more power to him.'"

Back home in San Francisco, Greg called up George McCown, the man whose birthday card he had delivered as he walked by the bridge to Korphe. McCown invited him to a special dinner given by the American Himalayan Foundation to honor Sir Edmund Hillary, who, along with Tenzing Norgay, had been part of the first team to climb Mount Everest. Greg said he'd see him there.

On September 13, 1995, Greg showed up at the fancy Fairmont Hotel. Wearing a brown sports coat that had been his father's, khakis, and beat-up leather shoes with no socks, he walked into a room filled with men in jackets and ties, women in black velvet dresses, and Tibetan Buddhist monks in cinnamon-colored robes.

Greg stood near the doorway, feeling lost. Then he spotted George McCown, talking with Jean Hoerni. George waved him over. Greg walked over to the men and hugged both of them.

"I just tell George he needs to give you some fund," Hoerni said in his French-accented English.

"Well, I should have enough already to finish the school, if I keep expenses down," Greg said.

"Not for the school," Hoerni answered. "For you. What are you supposed to live on while you get this place built?"

"How does twenty thousand sound?" McCown asked.

Greg couldn't answer.

"Shall I take that as an okay?" McCown said.

"Bring him a cocktail," Hoerni said, grinning. "I think Greg is about to faint."

Greg was stunned. He couldn't even remember much about the dinner afterward. The only thing he recalled was that the man sitting next to him was shocked to see that Greg wore no socks at such a formal dinner. He left the table and bought Greg a pair from the hotel gift shop.

But Greg was able to pay attention when Sir Edmund Hillary began to speak and show slides of his 1953 expedition to Everest. "I was just an enthusiastic mountaineer of modest abilities who was willing to work quite hard and had the necessary imagination and determination," he told the crowd. "I was just an average bloke. It was the **media** that tried to

Greg with Sir Edmund Hillary and Jean Hoerni at the American Himalayan Foundation dinner.

transform me into a heroic figure. But I've learned through the years, as long as you don't believe all that rubbish about yourself, you can't come to too much harm."

Greg's attention was caught even more when Hillary started showing slides of the work he had done since his record-breaking climb, building schools and medical clinics around Everest. Greg was so excited that he couldn't sit still. Getting up from the table, he paced back and forth in the rear of the room. He wanted to hear every word that Hillary said, and at the same time he wanted to get on the next plane that could take him toward Korphe so that he could get right to work.

"I have enjoyed great satisfaction from my climb of Everest. But my most worthwhile things have been the building of schools and medical clinics. That has given me more satisfaction than a footprint on a mountain," he heard Hillary say.

As Greg listened, he felt a tap on his shoulder and turned around. A pretty woman with short hair was smiling at him. Her name, he would learn, was Tara Bishop.

"I knew who Greg was," she explained later. "I'd heard about what he was trying to do, and I thought he had a great smile so I sort of sidled up to him." Whispering so they wouldn't interrupt Hillary's speech, the two of them began to talk. By the time the speech was over, Greg knew he was in love. "Tara had been wearing high heels, which I'd never really liked," he remembered. "At the end of the night her feet hurt, and she changed into a pair of combat boots. I don't know why that killed me, but it did. I felt like a teenager. Looking at her in

# Three Cups of Tea

that little dress and those big boots I was positive she was the woman for me."

At the end of the evening, they kissed for the first time.

"Welcome to my life," Tara said, pulling back to look Greg in the face.

"Welcome to my heart," he said, and wrapped her in his arms.

He left the hotel that night with the promise of a year's salary, arm in arm with the woman he would marry.

The next day, a Thursday, Tara drove Greg to the airport. He had tickets for a plane that would leave for Pakistan on Sunday, but together they told their story to the person working at the ticket counter, and persuaded her to change the flight for one a week later. She did it for free.

They spent every moment of the next few days together. On Saturday, the couple drove to Santa Cruz, California, to see Greg's cousin, Lana Pieri, and look at puppies. On the drive back on Sunday, Tara turned to look at Greg and asked, "So when are we getting married?"

"How's Tuesday?" Greg said.

On Tuesday, six days after they'd met, Greg and Tara got married at Oakland City Hall. They called up several friends, surprised them with the news, and told them to meet at an Italian restaurant to celebrate. One friend was James Bullock, the operator of a cable car, and he took the couple on a private tour of San Francisco. Arm in arm with his wife, Greg Mortenson watched dazzling views of the Pacific and the

64

Greg and Tara on their wedding day; September 16, 1996

Golden Gate Bridge. He realized that his cheeks felt tired, and then he understood why—he'd been smiling for days.

"When people hear how I married Tara, they're always shocked," he said. "But marrying her after six days doesn't seem strange to me. It's the kind of thing my parents did, and it worked for them. What's amazing to me is that I found the one person in the world I was meant to be with."

The next Sunday, Tara took Greg to the airport again. But after they parked, he couldn't make himself leave the car. He turned to his wife, who was grinning. "I'll ask," Greg said. "But I don't know if they'll let me do it again."

They did. Greg postponed his flight two more times.

The agents at British Airways had heard about his romantic marriage, and they bent the rules to give Greg more time to get to know his new wife. "It was a very special few weeks, a secret time," Greg remembered. "No one knew I was still in town, and we just barricaded ourselves inside Tara's apartment, trying to make up for all the years we hadn't known each other."

Finally, at the end of nearly three weeks together, Greg and Tara drove up to the airport once more. He kissed her good-bye and dragged his duffel bag to the ticket counter.

"You really want to go this time?" the ticket agent teased. "You sure you're doing the right thing?"

"Oh, I'm doing the right thing," Greg said, and turned to wave one last time at his wife. "I've never been this sure of anything."

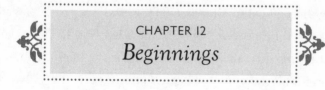

$B$ack in Skardu, Greg stood at the doorway to Changazi's office. A man with a club told him that Changazi was not there. When Greg held out the list of supplies that Changazi was supposed to be keeping, the man told him to come back in a month or two. Changazi would be back then. Then he tried to close the door.

Greg was trying to decide whether to insist on getting his supplies or to find a policeman when a dignified older man interrupted. His name was Ghulam Parvi, and he was an accountant Changazi had hired. Before coming to work for Changazi, he had been the director of a charity that had built two schools near Skardu. But the money had run out, and he'd been forced to take other jobs.

Now he looked at Greg and asked, in English, "Can I be of some assistance, sir?"

Greg handed him the receipt for the supplies and explained

what he needed them for. "I could waste my time with Changazi's **ledgers** for the next two weeks and still they would make no sense," said Parvi, wrapping a cream-colored scarf around his neck. "Shall we see what has become of your materials?"

They drove to a building about a mile outside town, where Changazi had stored the supplies for the school. But the building was fenced in, and the gate was locked. The next afternoon Greg and Parvi returned, and this time Parvi had a bolt cutter. But now someone else was there—a guard armed with a rifle. "You can't go in," the man said in Balti. "This building has been sold."

"This Changazi may wear white robes, but I think he is an exceedingly black-souled man," Parvi said to Greg. He turned to the guard and argued angrily, and at last the guard gave way. When Parvi was about to cut the lock off, the man even got out a key. Inside, Parvi and Greg discovered about two-thirds of the supplies that Greg had asked Changazi to keep. He would never manage to find the rest. But this would be enough to start with. With Parvi's help, he arranged for what remained of the wood, cement, and tin to be sent to Korphe by jeep.

"Without Parvi, I never would have accomplished anything in Pakistan," Greg said. "Parvi showed me how to get things done."

Before setting out for Korphe on a jeep himself, Greg shook Parvi's hand warmly and thanked him for his help. "Let me know if I can be of further assistance," Parvi said, with a slight bow. "What you're doing for the students of Baltistan is most laudable."

❦ ❦ ❦

Greg stood on a plain high above the Braldu River, gazing down at the site where Korphe's school was to be built. There was a pile of stones, looking like an ancient ruin. But the foundation, the floor, of the school was nowhere to be seen.

Looking at the site with Haji Ali, Greg struggled to hide his disappointment. It was mid-October. They should at least be building the walls this week, but they couldn't start the walls without the foundation. Soon winter would be here. No one could work in the cold weather. Greg kicked a stone angrily.

"What's the matter?" Haji Ali said in Balti.

Greg took a deep breath. "Why haven't you started?" he asked.

"Dr. Greg, we discussed your plan after you returned to your village," Haji Ali began. The chief explained that the villagers had decided it would be best if the men of Korphe cut the stone for the school themselves, instead of spending Greg's money to hire workers from other villages. "It took all summer, because many of the men had to leave for porter work," the village chief explained. "But don't worry. I have your money safely locked in my home."

"I'm not worried about the money," Greg said. "But I wanted to get a roof up before winter so the children would have someplace to study."

Haji put his hand on Greg's shoulder and gave his impatient

American friend a friendly squeeze. "I thank all-merciful Allah for all you have done. But the people of Korphe have been here without a school for six hundred years," he said, smiling. "What is one winter more?"

That night, lying on Haji Ali's roof next to Twaha, Greg thought of how lonely he'd been the last time he'd slept on this spot. He pictured Tara, remembering how she had waved at him through the airport window, and he couldn't keep his happiness to himself.

"Twaha, you awake?" Greg asked.

"Yes, awake."

"I have to tell you something. I got married."

Greg heard a click. Then he found himself squinting into the beam of the flashlight he'd brought as a present for his friend. Twaha sat up next to him, studying his face to see if he was joking.

Then he dropped the flashlight to the ground and pounded Greg on the arms and shoulders to congratulate him. Twaha collapsed onto his pile of blankets with a happy sigh. "Haji Ali say Dr. Greg look different this time," Twaha said, laughing. "He really know everything. Can I know her good name?"

"Tara."

"Ta . . . ra," Twaha said. "Ah yes, it means 'star' in our language . . . it's good a star come to make you happy. She is lovely, your Tara?"

"Yes," said Greg, blushing. "Lovely."

"How many goat and ram you must give her father?" Twaha

asked. In Balti culture, the bride's father must give the groom's family a bride price called a dowry—a payment of animals, sacks of flour, bags of sugar, and more—when two people get married.

"Her father is dead, like mine," Greg explained. "And in America, we don't pay a bride price."

"Did she cry when she left her mother?"

"She only told her mother about me after we were married."

Twaha was silent for a moment, considering the strange marriage customs of Americans.

The next morning, Sakina boiled an egg, a rare and precious item, for Greg's breakfast, and served it to him along with his *chapatti* and *lassi*. Haji Ali waited patiently while Greg finished his second cup of tea. Then he grinned. "Let's go build a school," he said.

After a prayer at the **mosque**, Haji Ali and Greg made marks on the ground where the walls of the school would go. Fifty men, including Greg, took turns with five shovels until they had dug a trench to be filled with cement. When the trench was done, six men carried two large stones over to the corner of the trench that faced Korphe K2. The stones had been specially carved to be cornerstones for the school.

Then Haji Ali called for the village's prize ram, the biggest and best male sheep. This animal, the most valuable one in the village, was killed as a sacrifice to bless the beginning of the school. The meat was shared with all the people of Korphe. "We didn't get anything else done that day," Greg said. "In fact, we hardly got anything else done that fall. . . . We just had a massive feast. For people who may only get meat a few times a year, that meal was a much more serious business than a school."

After the feast, Greg and a group of men built a large fire in what would one day be the courtyard of the finished school. They danced around the fire and sang traditional songs, while the women of the village clapped along. That night, Greg realized that, though he might not get to finish the school before he had to return home, it had finally become real to him.

🐝 🐝 🐝

By Thanksgiving, Greg was back in California. He and Tara spent the holiday with Jean Hoerni and his wife. "Listen," Hoerni said. "You love what you're doing in the Himalayas, and it doesn't sound like you're too bad at it. Why don't you make a career? The children of those other villages that try to bribe you need schools, too. . . . What if I **endowed** a foundation and made you the director? You could build a school every year. What do you say?"

Greg squeezed his wife's hand. The idea felt so right he was afraid to say anything. Afraid Hoerni would change his mind.

But Hoerni didn't. Many things changed for Greg over that winter. He and Tara left California and moved into a small house in Bozeman, Montana. Tara became pregnant. And Hoerni's foundation became a reality. By the time Greg returned to Pakistan in May, it was as the director of the **Central Asia Institute**, or the CAI.

K2, the world's second highest mountain

Greg at K2 Basecamp, Pakistan; 1993

Greg's sister Christa in Wyoming

Christa's amber necklace

The Korphe Bridge above the Braldu River; built 1995

Senior foreman Makmahl teaches Korphe kids masonry work; 1996

Mouzafer Ali, Greg's porte

Korphe men carry 80–120-lb. loads up the Braldu Valley after landslides block the road

Haji Ali, Korphe village chief and Greg's mentor; 1993

reg with Syed Abbas Risvi, head imam; 2007

Bedford truck's three-day trip to deliver school supplies

Korphe School is completed; 1996

Schoolteacher in Gultori war refugee girls' school, Balistan

Second-grader Nazir writes with a stick dipped in mud

Nasreen learns to sew in the Vocational Women's

Greg Mortenson

...efugees who fled artillery shelling during the India/Pakistan War

Jahan, the Braldu Valley's first educated woman

Yasmeen writes on a blackboard at an outdoor school for former Peshawar, Pakistan, refugees

Third-grade schoolgirl

Genevieve Chabot © 2008

Nazia and Sara carry water in Gultori war refugee camp, Skardu; 19

Refugee camp for earthquake victims in Azad Kashmir, Pakistan; 2005

Greg Mortenson

Earthquake refugees get clean water from a tank; 2005

Schoolboys in northern Pakistan where only 1 out of every 3 girls attends school

Schoolgirls in Batengi school, Azad Kashmir, Pakistan; 2008

Gultori war refugee students; 2007

Greg meets Mohammed in Korphe village; 1994

Ghulam Parvi

Greg greets a student at the opening of a girls' school in Chunda Village; 200

Greg at the Lalander School, which was once attacked by the Taliban; 2007

Sarfraz Khan

As director, he could afford to hire some help. Back in Pakistan, Greg contacted Mouzafer, the porter who had helped him make his way down from K2. He offered Mouzafer a steady salary if he'd come to Korphe to help with the school. Greg hired Ghulam Parvi as well. "I could see the greatness of Greg's heart right away," said Parvi. "We both wanted the same things for Baltistan's children. How could I refuse such a man?"

When he arrived in Korphe on a Friday afternoon, Greg crossed the bridge and was surprised to meet a group of Korphe's women, dressed in their best clothes, walking the other way. They were going to visit their families in neighboring villages. Without the bridge, it had been difficult for them to walk so far. Now that they could get there and back in an afternoon, the women started regular Friday visits to their families in other villages. "The bridge . . . made the women feel a whole lot happier and less isolated. Who knew that something as simple as a bridge could **empower** women?" Greg explains.

Haji Ali welcomed Greg back with a hug. Standing behind him was Mouzafer, looking as if he didn't feel well. Greg hugged him, too. "How are you?" he asked in Balti. He found out over dinner that, after the only road between Korphe and Skardu had been blocked by a landslide, Mouzafer had led a party of porters carrying ninety-pound bags of cement to the village. He had made the trip more than twenty times, skipping meals and walking day and night, so that the cement would be waiting when Greg arrived.

"When I first met Mr. Greg Mortenson on the Baltoro, he was a very friendly talking lad," Mouzafer said, "always joking and sharing his heart with the poor person like the porters. When I lost him and thought he might die out on the ice, I was awake all night, praying to Allah that I might be allowed to save him. And when I found him again, I promised to protect him forever with all my strength. I am poor, and can only offer him my prayer. Also the strength of my back. This I gladly gave him so he could build his school."

## CHAPTER 13
### *Haji Ali's Lesson*

The next morning, before it got light, Greg paced back and forth on the roof of Haji Ali's house. Now he was the director of a foundation, not just one climber trying to help one village. He had responsibilities. He owed it to Jean Hoerni to do this right. He was determined to get the school finished as quickly as possible.

Everyone gathered at the construction site. With dynamite, they blasted large boulders into smaller chunks of stone. Then dozens of people would carry the stones to **masons**, who would shape them into neat bricks with a few blows of a chisel. Women carried water from the river and used it to mix cement in large holes in the ground. The walls were built with the stone bricks and the cement, and children put slivers of stone into gaps between the bricks.

"We were all very excited to help," said Tahira, the daughter of Hussein, the teacher. She was ten years old when the

75

Ghulam carries 80-pound stone brick for Korphe School

construction began. "My father told me the school would be something very special, but I had no idea then what a school was, so I came to see what everyone was so excited about, and to help. Everyone in my family helped."

"Dr. Greg brought books from his country," said Haji Ali's granddaughter, Jahan, who was nine at the time. "And they had pictures of schools in them, so I had some idea of what we were helping to build. I thought Dr. Greg was very distinguished with his clean clothes. And the children in the pictures looked very clean, too. And I remember thinking, If I go to this school, maybe one day I can become distinguished, too."

All through June, the school walls rose steadily, but not fast enough for Greg. The men needed to take care of their crops and their animals, so they could not spend all their time on the school. Everything went slowly. "I spent all day at the construction site, from sunrise to sunset," Greg said. "I always had my notebook in my hand, and kept my eyes on everyone, anxious to account for every rupee. I didn't want to disappoint Jean Hoerni, so I drove people hard."

One day in August, Haji Ali appeared at the construction site. He tapped Greg on the shoulder and asked him to take a walk. He led the American up to a narrow ledge high above the village. Greg felt time slipping away, worried about all the tasks going on below that he couldn't supervise from here.

Haji Ali told Greg to look at the view. Icy mountain peaks knifed into the sky. Below them, Korphe, green with fields of ripening barley, looked small and vulnerable.

Haji Ali laid his hand on Greg's shoulder. "These mountains have been here for a long time," he said. "And so have we. You can't tell the mountains what to do. You must learn to listen to them. So now I am asking you to listen to me. By the mercy of Almighty Allah, you have done much for my people, and we appreciate it. But now you must do one thing more for me."

"Anything," said Greg.

"Sit down. And shut your mouth," said Haji Ali. "You're making everyone crazy."

"Then he reached out and took my plumb line and my level and my account book, and he walked back down to Korphe," Greg remembered. "I followed him all the way to his house, worrying about what he was doing. He took the key he always kept around his neck on a leather thong,

The Korphe School under construction; 1996

opened a cabinet decorated with faded Buddhist wood carvings, and locked my things in there. . . . Then he asked Sakina to bring us tea."

For half an hour, Greg fidgeted while Sakina brewed tea and Haji Ali looked through his **Koran**, the most precious thing he owned. When the cups of tea steamed in their hands, Haji Ali spoke. "If you want to thrive in Baltistan, you must respect our ways," he said, blowing on his tea. "The first time you share tea with a Balti, you are a stranger. The second time you take tea, you are an honored guest. The third time you share a cup of tea, you become family, and for our family, we are prepared to do anything, even die," he went on, laying a hand on Greg's own. "Dr. Greg, you must make time to share three cups of tea. We may be uneducated. But we are not stupid. We have lived and survived here a long time."

"That day, Haji Ali taught me the most important lesson I've ever learned in my life," Greg said. "We Americans think you have to accomplish everything quickly. . . . Haji Ali taught me to share three cups of tea, to slow down and make building relationships as important as building projects. He taught me that I had more to learn from the people I work with than I could ever hope to teach them."

🐸 🐸 🐸

Three weeks later, the walls of the school were as tall as Greg's head, and all that remained was to put on the roof. The original roof beams Greg had bought had not been found in Changazi's warehouse. Greg had returned to Skardu to buy new beams, with Parvi's help. But, not surprisingly, the road back to Korphe was blocked by a landslide. The jeeps carrying the beams could not get through.

But help showed up in the morning. "Haji Ali somehow heard about our problem, and the men of Korphe had walked all night," Greg said. "They arrived clapping and singing and in incredible spirits for people who hadn't slept." Greg was most amazed of all to see that Sher Takhi, the **mullah**, or religious leader, of Korphe had come along as well. Mullahs are not supposed to do physical labor. Their jobs are to pray, study, and teach. But Sher Takhi insisted on helping to carry the beams back to Korphe. "He wouldn't back down, and he led our column of thirty-five men carrying roof beams all the way, all eighteen miles to Korphe," Greg remembered. "Sher Takhi had **polio** as a child, and he walked with a limp, so it must have been agony for him. But he led us up the Braldu Valley, grinning under his load."

🐝 🐝 🐝

But not everyone was as pleased with the school as Sher Takhi. A week later, as Greg and Twaha stood watching the roof beams being laid into place, a band of men crossed the bridge and entered Korphe.

Greg followed Haji Ali out to see who the strangers were. Five men were approaching. One, who walked in front, seemed to be the leader. Four others walked behind him, carrying clubs that they smacked against their hands with each step.

Twaha leaned toward Greg. "This man Haji Mehdi. Not good," he whispered.

Greg already knew Haji Mehdi, the chief of Askole, and considered him a criminal. He demanded some of the money earned whenever any of the Balti sold a sheep, a goat, or a chicken. If someone in Askole sold supplies to mountain climbers and didn't give Haji Mehdi his share, the chief would send his men to beat them with clubs.

Haji Mehdi refused an invitation to drink tea. "I will speak out in the open, so you all can hear me," he said. "I have heard that an **infidel** has come to poison Muslim children, boys as well as girls, with his teachings. Allah forbids the education of girls. And I forbid the construction of this school."

"We will finish our school," said Haji Ali. "Whether you forbid it or not."

Greg hoped to calm things down. "Why don't we have tea and talk about this," he suggested.

"I know who you are, *kafir* [infidel]," said Mehdi. "And I have nothing to say to you." He turned to Haji Ali. "And you, are you not a Muslim? There is only one God. Do you worship Allah? Or this *kafir*?"

Haji Ali clapped his hand on Greg's shoulder. "No one else has ever come here to help my people. I've paid you money every year, but you have done nothing for my village. This man is a better Muslim than you. He deserves my devotion more than you."

"If you insist on keeping your *kafir* school, you must pay a price," Mehdi said. "I demand twelve of your largest rams."

"As you wish," Haji Ali said, turning his back on Mehdi,

to show how disgusted he was that the other chief had demanded a bribe. He ordered the villagers to bring out their prize rams.

"You have to understand, in these villages, a ram is like a firstborn child, prize cow, and family pet all rolled into one," Greg explained later. "The most sacred duty of each family's oldest boy was to care for their rams, and they were devastated."

Haji Ali took twelve of the rams and tied their bridles together. The boys who took care of the animals cried as they handed them over. He led the line of rams to Haji Mehdi and threw the lead rope to him without a word. Then he turned his back on the other chief and gathered the people of Korphe at the site of the school.

"It was one of the most humbling things I've ever seen," Greg said. "Haji Ali had just handed over half the wealth of the village to that crook, but he was smiling as if he'd won a lottery."

Haji Ali stood before the building everyone in Korphe had worked so hard to raise. It had snug stone walls, plastered and painted yellow, and thick wooden doors to keep out the wind. Never again would the children of Korphe kneel over their lessons on frozen ground. "Don't be sad," Haji Ali told the crowd. "Long after all those rams are dead and eaten this school will still stand. Haji Mehdi has food today. Now our children have education forever."

After dark that evening, by the fire in his house, Haji Ali beckoned Greg to sit beside him. He picked up his Koran. "Do you see how beautiful this Koran is?" he asked.

"Yes," Greg answered.

"I can't read it," he said. "I can't read anything. This is the greatest sadness in my life. I'll do anything so the children of my village never have to know this feeling. I'll pay any price so they have the education they deserve."

"Sitting there beside him," Greg said, "I realized that everything, all the difficulties I'd gone through, from the time I'd promised to build the school, through the long struggle to complete it, was nothing compared to the sacrifices he was prepared to make for his people. Here was this **illiterate** man, who'd hardly ever left his little village. . . . Yet he was the wisest man I'd ever met."

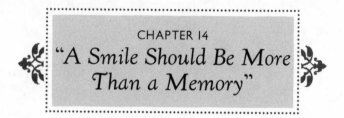

CHAPTER 14
## "A Smile Should Be More Than a Memory"

With the Korphe School nearly completed, Greg turned his attention elsewhere in his new role as director of the Central Asia Institute. He arrived in Peshawar, a city in the west of Pakistan, in August of 1996, looking for sites to build new schools. Peshawar is the capital of Pakistan's "wild west" and is full of rumors and news from nearby Afghanistan. A rebel group made up of mostly teenage students, the Taliban, had just attacked Afghanistan's government. They had taken over one large city, and rumors swirled through town of what else they had done. Some said they'd conquered the capital. Some said the leader of the government had left the country. Some said he'd been killed. No one really knew.

In the middle of this chaos, Osama bin Laden, the leader of a terrorist group called **Al Qaeda**, had arrived in Afghanistan. He planned to make the country his new home. The very week that Greg spent in Peshawar, bin Laden called on his followers to attack Americans wherever they could be found.

Greg didn't know about this. Like most Americans, he'd never heard of bin Laden. But he knew it was a dangerous time for a foreigner in Pakistan.

Haji Ali knew it, too. Before Greg had left Korphe, the chief had told him to be careful. "Promise me one thing," he'd said. "Don't go to any place alone. Find a host you trust, a village chief would be best, and wait until he invites you to his home to drink tea. Only in this way will you be safe."

But Greg didn't want to wait. Tara was pregnant, and the baby was due to be born in a month. He needed to check out possible sites for new schools and then get back to the United States. So he found a fellow guest in the hotel, a man named Badam Gul, who was from **Waziristan**, an area south of Peshawar. This man offered to guide Greg to his home village of Ladha. Greg accepted, even though he didn't know the man well. He was in a hurry.

Waziristan was the home of the Wazir tribe. Although the area is part of Pakistan, many people there don't have much loyalty to the country's government. Mostly they are loyal to their own tribe. Greg had read that the Wazirs were violent, not to be trusted, but then he had read similar things about the Balti. He thought it was more likely the Wazirs were simply outsiders, people the government of Pakistan didn't care much about, people who could probably use the kind of schools the new Central Asia Institute was going to build.

In the morning, Gul met Greg outside his hotel, but told

him that he'd been called away on business. Luckily, the driver of their car, a man named Mr. Khan, was from a small village near Ladha and could take Greg there. Greg briefly considered backing out, but he climbed into the car.

They drove through a desert landscape, past forts, factories where guns were made, and towns protected by twenty-foot walls with armed guards. At sunset, they arrived at Khan's village, Kot Langarkhel. Khan drove Greg to a large warehouse, and as they walked inside, Greg saw crates of guns and weapons stacked up around the walls, alongside boxes of Gatorade and Oil of Olay. He realized that he'd blundered into a large and well-organized smuggling operation.

All he could think of to do was to make the men inside the warehouse, the ones with large guns, think of him as a guest and not an enemy. He'd learned a few words of **Pashto**, the local language, from Khan on the drive down. He politely asked after the men's health and their families. They discussed what to do with him, and then Khan turned to his passenger. "Haji Mirza please to invite you his house," he said, referring to one of the smugglers. Greg finally relaxed. He'd be all right now. He was a guest.

They left the warehouse and climbed uphill for about half an hour until they reached Haji Mirza's home—a group of buildings protected by a twenty-foot wall and defended by a man with a rifle. The guard peered suspiciously at Greg, but he let him pass when Haji Mirza grunted.

Greg and Khan were led to a room with thick carpets and

cushions. They sipped tea and waited for two hours while dinner was prepared. After roasted lamb and rice with carrots, cloves, and raisins, Greg smoked a cigarette that he was handed, politely, as a good guest should. One of the men rolled out a mat for him to sleep on. He hadn't done so badly, Greg thought. He'd made contact with one tribal elder, at least, and tomorrow he'd ask to be introduced to others and find out how this village would feel about a school.

After only two hours of sleep, Greg was awakened by men shouting. Confused, he woke up to find a lamp in his face and a rifle pointed at his chest. Strangers with guns pulled him up by his arms, blindfolded him, and pulled him outside, where he was pushed into a pickup truck. "We drove for about forty-five minutes," Greg says. "I was finally fully awake, and I was shivering, partly because it was cold in an open truck in a desert. And also because now I was really afraid." As the truck jolted over the road, the men all around him argued in Pashto; he guessed they were discussing what his fate should be. But he couldn't understand them, and he also couldn't understand how these armed strangers had broken into Haji Mirza's house with all of his guards, without even firing a shot. Then he understood—his host had handed him over willingly.

The truck swerved off the highway, then stopped. Greg was pulled out onto the ground. He heard someone fumbling with a lock, then a metal gate swinging open. He was pushed inside, down a hallway, and through a door. His blindfold was removed.

He was in a simple room, ten feet by twenty, with a kerosene lamp burning on the single windowsill. He turned to say something to his kidnappers, but all he saw was the door closing behind them. He heard the sound of a padlock snapping shut.

There was a blanket and a pad on the dirt floor at the far end of the room. Despite his fear, Greg realized that it was better to sleep than worry. He lay down and slept dreamlessly. Greg woke in the morning to find two of his captors offering him tea. He did his best to talk to them, but they stayed near the door and ignored him. Hours passed. Greg dozed, woke, dozed again. "I began to get really depressed," Greg says. "I thought, 'This could go on for a very long time.'" Greg slipped in and out of sleep, finally waking to notice something on the floor beside his bed—a *Time* magazine.

He picked it up. It was seventeen years old, and it had a long article on the Iran hostage crisis. Greg read about the sixty-six Americans who had been taken hostage in Iran in 1979. The writer of the article didn't know it at the time, but it would be 444 days before the last of the hostages were finally released.

Would he be spending 444 days in this dim, bare room? The thought was horrifying. Greg decided to follow the lead of one of the hostages quoted in the article. She had been able to talk to one of her guards in his own language, and she thought that might have helped win her freedom. Greg decided that he *had* to find some way to communicate with these people who'd taken him prisoner.

The next day he asked for a Koran. His kidnappers brought

him one. The Koran was in Arabic, which Greg couldn't read, but he turned the pages carefully. After all, Haji Ali could not read his Koran, and he did the same. Five times a day, he prayed, as he'd been taught by the tailor in Rawalpindi on his second trip to Pakistan.

When he wasn't trying to read the Koran, Greg turned to the *Time* magazine. He decided not to read more about the Iran hostage crisis; it only made him more anxious. Instead, he studied the ads. Pictures of happy families in a new car (an ad for Chevrolet) or celebrating Christmas (Kodak Instamatic Cameras) held his attention for hours. They reminded him of home, of Tara, of their child, of everything waiting for him. During his sixth day of captivity, he found tears in his eyes as he looked at an ad for a WaterPik Oral Hygiene Appliance—a machine that squirted out a tiny jet of water to scour plaque away from teeth. The ad said, "A smile should be more than a memory."

As Greg was poring over pictures of a happy family with dazzling smiles, he sensed someone standing over his bed. He looked up to see a large man with a silvery beard and a kindly smile. The man greeted Greg in Pashto, and then said, "So you must be the American." In English.

Amazed, Greg stood up to shake his hand. The room spun around him. For the past few days, as he'd felt more and more depressed, he'd eaten nothing but rice and tea. Now he was dizzy from hunger. The man grabbed his shoulders, steadying him, and called for breakfast.

Between mouthfuls of warm *chapatti*, Greg made up for six days without speaking. When he asked the kindly man's name, the stranger paused for a moment before saying, "Just call me 'Khan.'" In Waziristan, "Khan" is as common as "Smith" in America. But Greg didn't care what the man wanted to be called, if he would only listen.

Over pots of green tea, he explained about the work he'd done in Baltistan and the many more schools he hoped to build for Pakistan's children. He'd come to Waziristan, he explained, to see if anyone here needed his help.

He hoped Khan would say that the whole thing had been a mistake, that he was free to go. But Khan simply picked up the *Time* magazine and looked through it. "My wife is about to give birth to our first child, a son," Greg added. "And I need to get home for his arrival."

Actually, the baby Tara was carrying would be a girl. Greg knew this. "But I knew that for a Muslim the birth of a son is a really big deal," he said later. "I felt bad about lying, but I thought that the birth of a son might make them let me go."

Khan continued to look through the magazine, frowning. "I told my wife I'd be home already," Greg continued. "I'm sure she's really worried. Can I telephone her to tell her I'm all right?"

"There are no telephones here," said Khan.

"What if you took me to one of the Pakistan army posts? I could call from there?"

Khan sighed. "I'm afraid that's not possible," he said. Then he looked Greg in the eye before gathering the tea things and taking his leave. "Don't worry," he said. "You will be just fine."

❧ ❧ ❧

Two days later, Khan appeared again. "You are a fan of football?" he asked.

"Sure," Greg said. He told Khan he'd played football in college. Only after he'd said it did he realize that Khan, who'd learned his English in a British school, meant the game that Americans call "soccer."

"Then we will entertain you with a match," Khan said, beckoning Greg toward the door. "Come."

Greg followed Khan out of the front gate and felt dizzy at the wide-open space all around him. He thought about making a run for it, but remembered that there was a man armed with a gun on a tall tower behind him. So instead, he sat in a small plastic chair and watched two dozen young, bearded men play a game of soccer on a wide, stony field. Their goalposts were made of stacked aluminum crates.

But before the game was over, the sentry on the tower called out. He'd seen some movement at a nearby army post. "Terribly sorry," Khan said as he herded Greg quickly back behind the compound's high walls.

That night, Greg couldn't sleep. Was the soccer match a sign that he'd be released soon? Or had they decided to let him have a few moments outside before they killed him?

When men arrived in his cell at four A.M., he thought he had his answer. Khan put a blindfold on Greg, draped a blanket over his shoulders, and led him outside to a pickup truck. Greg expected to be murdered. "I didn't think being shot was such a bad way to die," he said. "But the idea that Tara would have to raise our child on her own and would probably never find out what had happened to me made me crazy."

For the half hour that they drove, Greg pulled the blanket tightly around his shoulders, but he couldn't stop shivering. When the truck came to a stop and he could hear the sound of guns being fired, he broke out into a sweat.

But then Khan unwrapped Greg's blindfold and hugged him. "You see," he said. "I told you everything would work out for the best." Over Khan's shoulder, Greg saw hundreds of Wazir men dancing around bonfires, shooting off their guns, not in attack but in celebration. There were pots boiling and goats roasting over the flames.

"What is this?" he yelled, following Khan off the truck. "Why am I here?"

"It's best if I don't tell you too much," Khan settled. He told Greg that his fate had been decided by *jirga*, or a village council, and they were throwing a party. "A party before we take you back to Peshawar," Khan explained.

At first Greg didn't quite believe him. But he realized it was true when one of his former guards stumbled toward him, grinning, and stuffed a handful of rupee notes into the pocket of his *shalwar*.

"For your school!" Khan shouted in Greg's ear. "So, *Inshallah*, you'll build many more!"

CHAPTER 15
*A Picture*

$G$reg made it to Montana by September, just in time for the birth of his daughter, Amira Eliana. Amira was born at their home, and after her birth, Greg lay in bed with Tara and the baby, and placed the multicolored *tomar* that Haji Ali had given him around his daughter's neck.

But he couldn't stay in his cozy house with his wife and new daughter forever. Jean Hoerni called, demanding to know when Greg would have a picture of the completed Korphe School to show him. He was so impatient that Greg asked what was bothering him. Hoerni admitted that his doctors had told him he had **leukemia**, a cancer of the blood. He might live only a few more months. "I must see that school before I die," Hoerni said. "Promise me you'll bring me a picture as soon as possible."

"I promise," Greg said.

❦ ❦ ❦

Greg left the country only a few weeks after Amira's birth, determined to keep his promise to Hoerni. In Korphe it was clear and cold. Greg and the village men wrapped blankets over their *shalwars* and fitted the roof beams in place. It was too cold now to sleep on the rooftops, so Greg slept inside Haji Ali's house, along with the family and the animals they owned.

"We were all worried about Dr. Greg sleeping inside with the smoke and the animals, but he seemed to take no notice of these things," Twaha remembered. "We saw he had peculiar habits, very different from other Europeans. He made no demands for good food and environment. He ate whatever my mother put before him and slept in the smoke like a Balti. Due to Dr. Greg's excellent manners and he never tells a lie, my parents and I came to love him very much."

One evening Greg sheepishly confessed the story of his kidnapping in Waziristan to Haji Ali. "You went alone!" Haji Ali accused him. "You didn't seek the hospitality of a village chief! If you learn only one thing from me, learn this lesson well: Never go anywhere in Pakistan alone. Promise me that."

"I promise," Greg said.

"Where will you build your next school?" Haji Ali asked.

"I thought I'd travel to the Hushe Valley," Greg said. "Visit a few villages and see who—"

"Can I give you some advice?" Haji Ali interrupted.

"Sure."

"Why don't you leave it to us? I'll call a meeting of all the elders of the Braldu and see what village is ready to donate free land and labor for a school. That way you don't have to flap all over Baltistan like a crow again, eating here and there," Haji Ali said, laughing.

"So once again, an illiterate old Balti taught a Westerner how to best go about developing his 'backward' area," Greg said later. "Ever since then, with all the schools I've built, I've remembered Haji Ali's advice and expanded slowly, from village to village and valley to valley, going where we'd already built relationships, instead of trying to hopscotch to places where I had no contacts, like Waziristan."

❦ ❦ ❦

By early December, the windows in the Korphe School were in place and blackboards were hung inside. On the afternoon of December 10, 1996, Greg crouched on the roof with Twaha, Hussein, and the rest of the workers, and pounded in the last nail. The first snowflakes of the season swirled down. Haji Ali cheered from the ground. "I asked almighty Allah to delay the snow until you were done," he said, grinning, "and in his infinite wisdom he did. Now come down and take some tea!"

That evening, Haji Ali unlocked the cupboard inside his house and gave Greg back his level and plumb line. Then he handed him a notebook. Greg turned the pages, amazed to see rows of numbers. "The village had accounted for every rupee spent on the school, adding up the cost of every brick, nail, and board, and the wages paid to put them together," he said. "And they did a much better job of it than I ever could have."

❦ ❦ ❦

Back in the United States, Greg drove from Montana, through a blizzard, to reach the hospital in Hailey, Idaho, where Jean Hoerni was staying. The snow made driving slow, and he finally got there at two A.M. Hoerni was awake, sitting up in bed. "You're late," he said. "Again." When Greg asked how he was feeling, he didn't answer. He just wanted to know if Greg had brought him a picture of Korphe's school.

Greg put an envelope into his hands and watched his face as he opened it.

Jean Hoerni pulled out an eight-by-ten photograph of Korphe School that Greg had taken the day he left. "*Magnifique* [magnificent]!" he said, nodding at the sturdy, pale-yellow building with fresh crimson trim. He traced his finger along the line of seventy ragged, smiling students who were about to begin their education safe, warm, and indoors for the first time.

The completed Korphe School

Hoerni called a nurse and asked him to bring him a hammer and nail. All she could get was a stapler. Greg pulled a watercolor picture of two kittens off the wall and stapled the picture of the school up where Hoerni could see it from his bed.

Greg turned back to Hoerni and saw him on the phone with an overseas operator. He was calling a childhood friend in Switzerland. "It's me, Jean," he said in French. "I built a school in the Karakoram," he boasted. "What have you done for the last fifty years?"

🐸 🐸 🐸

For the last few weeks of Hoerni's life, Greg became his nurse. It was the final time he would work as a nurse, and he was glad he knew how to make his friend comfortable. He also hooked up a video camera to the hospital television and showed Hoerni movies he'd taken of village life in Pakistan. Hoerni lay in bed, holding Greg's hand, watching as Korphe's children sang "Mary Had a Little Lamb" in their less-than-perfect English. "Jean didn't go quietly. He was angry about dying," Greg said. But as he watched the children sing, his anger drained away. He said to Greg, "I love you like a son."

Before he went into the hospital, Hoerni gave the Central Asia Institute one million dollars. He wanted to ensure that the organization was on solid ground—just like the Korphe School. After he died, in January of 1997, the institute would be able to continue the vision that Hoerni and Greg had started together.

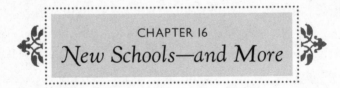

$G$reg set up an office for the Central Asia Institute, or the CAI, in the basement laundry room of his house. Since there is a time difference of twelve hours between Pakistan and Montana, where he now lived, he would make his first calls of the day around nine at night, to catch people in the morning in Pakistan. Then he'd go to sleep for a few hours, waking at two or three in the morning to make more calls, reaching people in Pakistan before they went home for the day. One of the first people he hired to work for the Institute was Ghulam Parvi, who'd helped him get the supplies for Korphe's school out of the hands of Changazi. Mouzafer also worked for the CAI now, along with Haji Ali, Twaha, and other people Greg had met in his travels in Pakistan.

It had taken three years to get Korphe's school completed. But the Central Asia Institute finished its next three schools in three months, including one in Changazi's village of Kuardu.

And it built more than schools. While Greg was spending some time in Korphe, meeting with Haji Ali, Twaha, and Hussein, two women approached them. Sakina, Haji Ali's wife, and Hawa, Hussein's wife, boldly sat down with the men. "We appreciate everything you're doing for our children," Hawa said. "But the women want me to ask you for something more."

Life in winter was hard for the women in Korphe, Hawa and Sakina explained. Trapped inside their homes by the freezing weather, they had little to do and no chance to talk to each other. "Allah willing, we'd like a center for the women, a place to talk and sew," Hawa said.

By the summer of 1997, an unused back room in Haji Ali's house had become the Korphe Women's **Vocational** Center. With four new sewing machines and lessons from a nearby tailor, the women of Korphe had a place where they could gather and work to help them earn a little money for their families.

That summer, Greg, Tara, and Amira, just eight months old, traveled to Pakistan. In August, they traveled up to Korphe for a ceremony to celebrate the school's opening. "It was incredible to finally see the place Greg had talked so passionately about for years," Tara says. "The day of the inauguration, we met Haji Ali and his wife, and the whole village competed to take turns holding Amira."

The school had been freshly painted for the occasion and hung with banners and Pakistani flags. There were new wooden desks, thick carpets to protect the children's feet from the cold, and books to make a school library. Jean Hoerni's widow was there to give each child a new school uniform.

"It was the most exciting day of my life," said Tahira, the daughter of Hussein. "Mr. Parvi handed each of us new books and I didn't dare to open them, they were so beautiful. I'd never had my own books before."

Twaha's daughter, Jahan, was excited, too. "I couldn't take my eyes off all the foreign ladies," she said. "They seemed so dignified." Before the school opened, when she'd seen people from "downside," or below the mountains, she'd felt shy. "I'd run away," she explained, "ashamed of my dirty clothes. But that day I held the first set of clean, new clothes I'd ever owned. And I remember thinking, Maybe I shouldn't feel so ashamed. Maybe one day, Allah willing, I can become a great lady, too."

There were speeches from Haji Ali, from Hussein and the two other teachers who'd been hired to work with him, and from many others who'd come to see Korphe's school. But one person didn't speak—Greg Mortenson. "While the speeches went on, Greg stood in the background, against the wall," Tara remembered, "holding a baby somebody had handed him. It was the most filthy baby I'd ever seen, but he didn't seem to notice. He just stood there happily, bouncing it in his arms."

Greg showed Tara and Amira around Baltistan. After his wife and daughter returned to the United States, he stayed two months more to help organize a new project. With the help of Mouzafer and Tara's brother, a climber who'd reached the peak of Everest, Greg created a school for Balti porters. They were trained in climbing, administering first aid, and rescuing people who were lost or injured. The school also tried to repair some of the damage to the environment done by climbing expeditions. Every year they organized a trip to take away tin cans, glass, and plastic trash from base camps in the mountains. The camps were cleaned up and the porters sold the recyclable materials, earning some extra money that they badly needed.

Word of what the Central Asia Institute was doing spread. When Greg returned to Skardu the next spring, people arrived at his hotel to talk to him or hand him badly spelled notes asking for help with anything from starting a mining business to rebuilding a mosque. He didn't have time to speak with everybody who came to see him, and he started to eat his meals in the hotel kitchen, hiding out where no one could find him. He sorted through all the notes and requests, trying to find the projects that the CAI could handle.

Greg also came to know a religious leader in Baltistan, Syed Abbas Risvi, who agreed with him that education was important but pointed out that the children in the area needed something else, too—clean water. In some villages, he said, more than a third of the children died before they were a year old, many because they didn't have clean water to drink or bathe in. Greg agreed that this was something the CAI should help with. After all, a plant had to be watered before it could grow, and children had to survive long enough to be able to go to school.

With Syed Abbas, Greg visited the chief of a village called

Chunda, and asked for the help of the people there. Four nearby villages heard what was happening and asked to join in. With hundreds of workers digging for ten hours a day, trenches were finished and pipes were put in place to bring fresh spring water to the villages.

The CAI planned to build three more schools in the summer of 1998. Greg was most interested in the school for Mouzafer's village. Mouzafer was not as strong as he once had been. He had seemed to grow old all at once, and was getting more and more deaf.

Greg found a piece of open land in Mouzafer's village, between two groves of apricot trees. Three months later, a school was standing there. Despite his age, Mouzafer carried rocks to the construction site and raised roof beams into place.

Standing with Greg in front of the finished school, as the children peered on tiptoe through the glass windows at the mysterious rooms where they'd begin getting their education in the fall, Mouzafer took his friend's hands.

"I'd like to work with you for many more years," he said, "but Allah, in his wisdom, has taken much of my strength."

Greg hugged him. "What will you do now?" he asked.

Mouzafer said he would spend his time working in the gardens and orchards of his town. "My work now," he explained simply, "is to give water to the trees."

❧ ❧ ❧

One June day in 1998, Greg was trying to start a new school to be built in Khane, the village where his K2 expedition coo lived. But arguments were still going on there over what kind of school he should build—a climbing school or a school for children. As Greg was trying to sort things out, a man bumped up in a borrowed jeep. He introduced himself as the chief of a village called Hushe. "I've been trying to meet you for one year now," he said. "Please, in evening time, you come to Hushe and attend our tea party."

❦ ❦ ❦

The chief's name was Mohammed Aslam Khan. When he was a boy, his father had woken him up early one morning and told him that he was leaving the village. "Why do I have to go?" Aslam asked, crying.

"You're going to school," his father said.

Aslam's father walked with him down their mountain until the trail ended at a river with no bridge. Aslam couldn't swim, but he clung to goat bladders blown full of air to stay afloat and kicked his way across the icy water. A stranger on the far bank pulled him out and wrapped him in a blanket as he shivered and cried. When Aslam told the stranger that he'd crossed the river to go to school, the man comforted him.

"Don't be afraid," he said. "You're a brave boy to come so far from home. One day, you'll be honored by everyone when you return."

Alone, Aslam made his way to a large town and was enrolled in a government school. When he graduated years later, he was at the top of his class. He was offered a job in government, but turned it down to return to Hushe and become the chief of his village. He got the government of Pakistan to build a road to Hushe and even a school, so that other children would not have to leave home as he had done to get an education. But the building was badly constructed. And only the boys could study there.

"I have been blessed nine times," Aslam says. "With five boys and four girls. But my daughter Shakeela is the most clever. There was nowhere for her to pursue her studies, and she was too young to send away. . . . I began to hear rumors about a big Angrezi who was building schools that welcomed boys and girls all over Pakistan. I decided to seek him out." Aslam was surprised after meeting Greg. "I expected to have to plead with an Angrezi Sahib like a little man," he said. "But he spoke to me as a brother. I found Greg a very kind, softhearted, naturally pleasing man. Every year since we built our school this feeling gets stronger, and finally, that love has spread to all my children and all the families of Hushe."

After sipping butter tea and talking with Aslam deep into the night, Greg agreed to give up the idea of a school in Khane and build one in Hushe instead. In 1998, the year it was finished, Aslam's daughter Shakeela was eight years old. "At first, when I began to attend school, many people in the village told me a girl has no business doing such a thing," Shakeela said. "They said you will end up working in the fields, like all women, so why fill your head with the foolishness found in books? But I knew how much my father valued education, so I tried to shut my mind to the talk and I persisted in my studies." After sh

Aslam with Shakeela, the Hushe Valley's first educated woman

finished Hushe school, where she was the top student, Shakeela left home to go to high school, the first girl in her town to move beyond elementary school.

Greg realized that more of Pakistan's girls needed a chance like Shakeela's. "Once you educate the boys, they tend to leave the villages and go search for work in the cities," he said. "But the girls stay home, become leaders in the community, and pass on what they've learned." He told the villages where the CAI had built schools that they must get more girls in the classrooms, ten percent more every year, in order to keep getting help from the CAI. "If the girls can just get to a fifth-grade level," he said, "everything changes."

Things were certainly different in Shakeela's village. She could see that for herself. "People's minds in Hushe are beginning to change," she said. "Now, when I return to my village, I see all the families sending their girls to school. And they tell me, 'Shakeela, we were mistaken. You were right to read so many books and brave to study so far from home. You're bringing honor to the village.'" Shakeela dreams of going on to medical school and becoming a doctor. "I've learned the world is a large place," she said. "And so far, I've only seen a little of it."

Holding a test on which his daughter had gotten a perfect score, Aslam said, "For these blessings, I thank Almighty Allah and Mr. Greg Mortenson."

## CHAPTER 17
### Running from War

For as long as Greg had been coming to Pakistan, the country had been fighting with its neighbor, India, over the region of **Kashmir**. Both India and Pakistan claimed Kashmir for their own. In 1999, the fighting became more serious. Troops moved into position, and fighter jets started bombing the area. **Refugees** from Kashmir, fleeing the bombs and **artillery shells** the armies were aiming at each other, began to pour into Baltistan.

Greg bought a plane ticket.

When he arrived, Greg spoke with Syed Abbas. He'd never seen the mullah so upset. No one knew how many people had been injured or killed by the bombing, he said, but two thousand refugees had already reached Skardu. Thousands of others were still near their homes, hiding in caves, waiting for the worst of the fighting to be over. Then they would flee Kashmir as well. Syed Abbas had contacted several international organizations to ask for help. But the organizations turned him down, and the local government didn't have the money or the supplies to help them.

"What do the people need?" Greg asked.

"Everything," Syed Abbas said. "But most of all, water."

Together, Syed and Greg went to see the refugees. Most of the refugees in Skardu were men who had left their families to come to make new homes where their wives and children could join them. They had been allowed to set up tents on land nobody else wanted, sand dunes next to the airport. There was no source of water there, and the nearest river was more than an hour's walk away. Greg's head throbbed. This was a huge task. "How can we bring water here?" he asked. "We're a long way uphill from the river."

Syed Abbas thought that if they drilled deep into the ground, they might be able to pump water up. His black robes billowed as he ran ahead over the bright sand, pointing out places where he thought they might look for water deep underground. "I wish that Westerners who misunderstand Muslims could have seen Syed Abbas in action that day," Greg said. "They would see that most people who practice the true teachings of Islam, even conservative mullahs like Syed Abbas, believe in peace and justice, not in terror."

While Greg and Abbas discussed water, another CAI worker, Apo Razak, walked among the tents, talking to people, making lists of urgently needed supplies. There were more than fifteen hundred hungry refugees in the camp, but everyone realized that soon the number could grow to four or five thousand. Now

Greg Mortenson

Syed Abbas Risvi; 2006

Apo came up to the other two men, his face serious. "Dr. Greg," he said, taking Greg's hand and leading him toward the tents, "enough talking. How can you know what the people need if you don't ask them?"

Apo led Greg to a tent. Inside sat Mullah Gulzar, the religious leader of a village called Brolmo. He shook Greg's hand and apologized for not being able to make him any tea. When they were all seated cross-legged on the warm sand, the mullah told his story.

"We didn't want to come here," Mullah Gulzar said, stroking his beard. "Brolmo is a good place. Or it was. We stayed as long as we could, hiding in the caves by day and working the fields at night. If we had worked by day, none of us would have survived, because there were so many shells falling. Finally, all the **irrigation channels** were broken, the fields were ruined, and the houses were shattered. We knew our women and children would die if we didn't do something, so we walked over the mountains to Skardu. I'm not young, and it was very difficult.

"When we came to the Skardu town, the army told us to make our home here," he went on. "And when we saw this place, we decided to go home. But the army would not permit it. They said, 'You have no home to go back to. It is broken.' Still, we would return if we could, for this is not a life. And now our women and children will soon come to this wasteland, and what can we tell them?"

Greg took the mullah's hand in both of his. "We will help you bring water here for your families," he promised.

"Thanks to Allah Almighty for that," the mullah said. "But water is only a beginning. We need food, and medicine, and education for our children. This is our home now. I'm ashamed to ask for so much, but no one else has come." The old man's eyes were damp with tears. "And we have nothing. For your *mal-la khwong*, for your kindness in fulfilling our prayers, I can offer you nothing," Mulllah Gulzar said. "Not even tea."

With money from the CAI, pipes and bulldozers from Skardu, twelve tractors loaned by the army, and work from the villagers of Brolmo, Greg fulfilled his promise. After drilling down 120 feet, they hit water that could be pumped up to fill a tank for the camp. Now the men of Brolmo could start building mud-block houses for their families. But first the women and children had to survive their journey to Skardu.

Fatima Batool was one of the children of Brolmo. She and her sister Aamina had run for shelter in caves after bombs and shells had destroyed their homes and fields. A shell had landed near Aamina before she could reach the caves. She hadn't been badly injured, but since then, she had not spoken a word. When she heard a shell explode, she would shake and whimper.

"Life was very cruel in the caves," said Fatima's friend Nargiz Ali. "Our village, Brolmo, was a very beautiful place, with apricot and even cherry trees, on a slope by the Indus River. But we could only glance out at it and watch it being destroyed."

After a while the few men who had stayed in the caves decided that the time had come to be brave and leave. They took what little food they could find in the ruins of their homes and walked away in the middle of the night. The next morning, out in the open, they were cooking bread over a fire when artillery shells began to fall near them again.

"Every time a shell exploded, Aamina would shake and cry and fall to the earth," Fatima explained. "In that place there were no caves, so all we could do is run. I'm ashamed to say that I was so frightened that I stopped tugging at my sister and ran to save myself. I was fearful that she would be killed, but being alone must have been more frightening to my sister than the shelling, and she ran to join the rest of the village."

For three weeks, the survivors of Brolmo walked northwest, finding their way on paths made by animals, eating whatever berries and wild plants they could find, always hungry. At last they arrived in Skardu, and the dunes by the airport. But it was too late for Aamina. "When we reached our new village, Aamina lay down and would not get up," Fatima says. "No one could revive her, and not even being safe at last with our father and uncles seemed to cheer her. She died after a few days."

Nothing would ever make up to the refugees for the loss of their homes and so many members of their families. But Fatima's friend Nargiz remembers one good thing that happened after they reached Skardu. "When we arrived after our long walk, we were, of course, very happy to see our families," she said. "But then I looked at the place where we were supposed to live, and I felt frightened and unsure. There were no houses. No trees. No mosque . . . Then Syed Abbas brought a large *Angrezi* to talk with us. He told us that if we were willing to work hard, he would help us build a school. And do you know, he kept his *chat-ndo*, his promise."

Fatima and Nargiz both attend the Gultori Girls Refugee School, built by the CAI and located near the Skardu airport. (Their brothers walk into town each day to go to a government school.) This is the first and only school the girls have ever been to. Because they started their education late, most students are fifteen by the time they graduate from fifth grade.

"I've heard some people say that Americans are bad," Fatima said. "But we love Americans. They are the most kind people for us. They are the only ones who cared to help us."

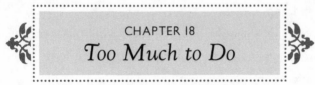

Building new schools and providing teachers and educations to isolated villages and refugee camps costs money. Despite Jean Hoerni's generosity, the CAI needed more funds to continue on. Greg began to give talks about the work the CAI was doing. With a slide projector held together with duct tape, he traveled the country. He'd leave envelopes on the audience's chairs, and after he spoke, he'd gather them up, usually with donations inside. He hated getting up in front of an audience to talk about himself, but the one or two hundred dollars he collected each time made it worthwhile. He knew how that money could help the children of Pakistan.

But this time it looked like he wouldn't get much for his efforts. He was scheduled to give a talk about the CAI at a sports store in Apple Valley, Minnesota. But it was nearly a half hour after the time he was supposed to start, and nobody had sat down.

Then two of the store's employees showed up and took seats in the last row. "What should I do?" Greg said. "Should I still give my talk?"

They said he should. So Greg started in, presenting his slide show to two people and 198 empty chairs. He showed pictures of K2 and talked about his climb. Then he began to talk about the CAI. Slides flashed on the screen of the eighteen schools the CAI had built. As Greg spoke about the schools and told stories about the children who went there—including Fatima, Nargiz, and their classmates—he caught the eye of a middle-aged man nearby who was quietly looking at a display of digital watches. Greg smiled, and the man sat down in the last row as well.

Now with three people to talk to, Greg went on for half an hour more. He talked about the terrible **poverty** the children of Pakistan endure. He talked about the CAI's plan to begin building new schools at the northern edge of Pakistan, along the border it shares with Afghanistan. He finished by quoting Mother Teresa, a Catholic nun who spent many years in India, working to improve the lives of the poor. "What we are trying to do may be just a drop in the ocean," he said, smiling warmly at his small audience. "But the ocean would be less because of that missing drop."

As Greg finished, his three listeners applauded. The two store employees helped him stack up the empty chairs and pick up the empty envelopes Greg had laid on them. One of the workers offered Greg a ten-dollar bill. He'd been planning to spend the money going out with his friends after work, he said, but if the CAI could use it . . .

"Thanks," Greg said, shaking his hand and putting the money into an envelope. Then he went back to picking up the rest of the empty envelopes.

On the last seat of the last chair in the last row, next to the display of digital watches, was an envelope with a check inside for twenty thousand dollars.

❦ ❦ ❦

Greg didn't collect twenty thousand dollars every time he gave a talk. But he didn't usually face a sea of empty seats either. Especially in the Pacific Northwest—Oregon, Washington, Idaho, and Montana—he was becoming well known. Some newspapers and magazines wrote about his story. Mountain climbers, in particular, became strong supporters of the CAI. Alex Lowe, a famous mountaineer, introduced Greg at one event. "While most of us are trying to scale new peaks," he told the audience, "Greg has been quietly moving even greater mountains on his own. . . . His kind of climb is one we should all attempt." In some places, when Greg Mortenson gave a speech, people were turned away because there were not enough seats.

Even so, some people at the CAI were getting frustrated with Greg. He knew how to climb mountains, knew how to get schools built, but he wasn't much of a businessman. The CAI had a board, a group of people who were supposed to decide which projects to work on and how money should be spent.

But Greg often got so busy that he didn't return the board members' phone calls or e-mails. They wouldn't hear from him for weeks.

Even though he was busy, Greg also didn't want to use up precious money to hire anybody to help. He thought he could handle every project himself—but the work was too much. He didn't have enough time for every project. And he wasn't taking care of himself, either—not sleeping, not exercising. "I understand that he decided to pour everything into his work," one CAI board member said. "But if he drops dead of a heart attack, what then?"

Tara agreed with some of what people at the CAI were saying about her husband. She called a meeting with her husband at the kitchen table.

"I told Greg I love how passionate he is about his work," she said. "But I told him he had a duty to his family, too. He needed to get more sleep, get some exercise, and get enough time at home to have a life with us." She and Greg agreed that he wouldn't go to Pakistan for longer than two months at a time.

Greg also began training himself to become a better manager of the CAI. He spent time in his basement, reading books on management and finance. But he knew some lessons couldn't be learned from books. So he also traveled to Bangladesh and to the Philippines, hoping to learn from other organizations that helped the poor. He was very impressed with the schools that had been built for girls in Bangladesh, one of the poorest countries on Earth. "The girls' education **initiative** is hugely successful there,"

Greg says. He visited the places that had been educating girls for a long time. "I watched as amazing, strong women held village meetings and worked to empower their daughters."

"They were following the same philosophy I was," he said. "**Nobel Prize** winner Amartya Sen's idea that you can change a culture by giving its girls the tools to grow up educated so they can help themselves. It was amazing to see the idea in action, working so well after only a generation, and it fired me up to fight for girls' education in Pakistan."

🐝 🐝 🐝

In September 1997, during one of those trips, Greg's flight back to the United States stopped briefly in Calcutta, India. There, he learned that one of his heroes, Mother Teresa, had died. A nun who had dedicated her life to serving "the poorest of the poor," she had founded her own **order**, the Sisters of Charity. Their duty, she said, was to care for "the hungry, the naked, the homeless, the crippled, the blind, the lepers, all those people who feel unwanted, unloved, uncared for throughout society, people that have become a burden to the society and are shunned by everyone."

Greg headed to where Mother Teresa lay, among hundreds of quiet mourners. A young nun led him to the room where Mother Teresa's body was. He sat in a corner, looking at her body, covered by a shroud. Greg says he had "no idea what to do. Since I was a little boy, she'd been one of my heroes. She looked so small, draped in that cloth," he said. "And I remember thinking how amazing it was that such a tiny person had such a huge effect on humanity."

❦ ❦ ❦

Even two years later, back home in the winter of 1999, alone in his basement office, Greg often thought of Mother Teresa and all she had accomplished. He himself was feeling tired and frustrated. He ignored the ringing phone and the e-mails that piled up, and focused on reading more and more about a tragedy on the borders of Afghanistan.

More than ten thousand Afghan refugees, mostly women and children, had fled from the Taliban rebels who had taken over the government of their country. Finally they reached the border between Afghanistan and **Tajikistan**. Soldiers on the Tajik side would not let them in; the Taliban would not let them go back. On islands in the middle of a river, they lived in mud huts and ate grass, slowly starving.

"Since I started working in Pakistan, I haven't slept much," Greg said. "But that winter of 1999 and 2000, I hardly slept at all. I was up all night, pacing my basement, trying to find some way to help them."

Greg wrote letters to the newspaper, to the president, to Congress, trying to get someone to help the refugees. "But no one cared," Greg said. "Bottom line is, I failed. I couldn't make anyone care. And Tara will tell you I was a nightmare. All I could think about was all those freezing children who'd never have a chance to grow up, helpless out there between groups of men with guns. . . . I was actually going a bit crazy. It was amazing that Tara put up with me that winter.

"In times of war," he went on, "you often hear leaders—

Christian, Jewish, and Muslim—saying, 'God is on our side.'
But that isn't true. God is on the side of refugees, widows, and
orphans."

But on July 24, 2000, Greg's spirits lifted. That day Tara
gave birth to their son, Khyber Bishop Mortenson, at home.
Greg felt happy for the first time in months. Later, he wrapped
his son in a fuzzy blanket and brought him to Amira's preschool
class for show-and-tell.

Amira proudly showed off her new baby brother's tiny
fingers and toes. "He's so small and wrinkly," said one of
Amira's classmates, a blond four-year-old. "Do little babies like
that grow up to be big like us?"

"*Inshallah*," Greg said.

"Huh?"

"I hope so, sweetie," Greg said. "I sure hope so."

On September 10, 2001, Greg and George McCown were
headed for a town called Zuudkhan, at the very tip of northern
Pakistan, near the border with Afghanistan. It was the
hometown of Faisal Baig, who had been a porter on McCown's
expedition to K2 and afterward came to work for the CAI as
Greg's bodyguard. The CAI had paid for three improvements
there: a water project, a small power plant, and a **dispensary**,
where medicine could be given out to villagers who needed
it. George McCown, who had donated eight thousand dollars
toward the projects in Zuudkhan, was traveling with Greg,
McCown's son Dan, and Dan's wife Susan, to see what the
CAI had done.

Zuudkhan's mud-brick houses matched the color of the
valley floor. It was hard to see the town until they were almost
on top of it. On the polo field, Faisal Baig was standing proudly
among a crowd of villagers, waiting to welcome his guests.

Baig lifted McCown off the ground in a bone-crushing hug. "Faisal is a true gem," McCown said. "We'd stayed in touch ever since my trip to K2, when he got me and my bum knee down the Baltoro and practically saved the life of my daughter Amy, who he carried most of the way down after she got sick. There in his home village he was so proud to show us around. He organized a royal welcome."

Musicians blowing horns and banging drums led the visitors down a line of all three hundred people in Zuudkhan. Greg had been to the village several times before and was greeted like family. The men hugged Greg and the women kissed him in the traditional way, laying their palms on his cheek and kissing the backs of their own hands.

Greg and McCown looked at the pipes that carried water to the town from a mountain stream and switched on the small **generator** powered by the water. The generator created enough electricity to light lamps in a few dozen houses for a couple of hours every evening. The two men also visited the new dispensary, where Aziza Hussain, the first health care worker in Zuudkhan, had just returned from six months of training. Now, with the simple medical supplies that the CAI had paid for, she hoped to be able to help people with illnesses that could be easily treated, but had been deadly before, simply because there were no doctors or clinics nearby.

Before Aziza took charge of health care in her village, many people had died. "After I got training and Dr. Greg provided the medicines . . . with good water from the new pipes, and teaching the people how to clean their children, and use clean food, not a single person has died here from these problems," says Aziza. "It's my great interest to continue to develop myself in this field. And pass on my training to other women. Now that we have made such progress, not a single person in this area believes women should not be educated."

🌱 🌱 🌱

The next day was September 11, 2001. Everyone gathered at a stage set up at the edge of the polo ground. Village elders performed a traditional dance of welcome, and Greg got up to dance with them. The entire village howled in appreciation. There were endless speeches, some by students in Zuudkhan's school, proud to display their skill in English. "We were lonely here in Zuudkhan," one boy said. "But Dr. Greg and Mr. George wanted to improving our village. For the benefit of the poor and needy of this world like the Zuudkhan people, we tell our benefactors thank you." The ceremonies finished up with a polo match. The players rode bareback on horses and tried to hit the goat skull used as a ball into the goals.

At four-thirty the next morning, Baig shook Greg awake. He had a portable radio pressed against his ear. Greg saw an expression on Baig's face that he had never seen there before—fear.

"Dr. Sahib! Dr. Sahib! Big problem," Baig said. "Up! Up!"

"As-salaam alaikum, Faisal," Greg said. "How are you?"

"I'm sorry," Baig said.

"Why?" Greg asked.

"A village called New York has been bombed."

Greg pulled a yak-hair blanket over his shoulders and stepped outside. Baig's brother was there with a gun, guarding his American guests. The village mullah stood outside also, looking toward Afghanistan. A friend of Baig's fiddled with his radio, trying to get more news. All anybody could figure out was that there had been a terrorist attack, and the two towers of the World Trade Center in New York had fallen.

"Your problem in New York village comes from there," Baig said. He spat toward Afghanistan. "From Osama."

A helicopter arrived in Zuudkhan shortly after to pick up Greg, McCown, and his family. It was sent by Brigadier General Bashir Baz, who had retired from Pakistan's army to run an air charter company, flying people around Pakistan. Since he'd learned of Greg Mortenson's work, he'd volunteered his planes and pilots to bring Greg to the remote corners of Pakistan. "I've met a lot of people in my life, but no one like Greg Mortenson," Bashir said. "Taking into account how hard he works for the children of my country, offering a flight now and then is the least I can do."

Guards with guns jumped out and helped the Americans into the helicopter. Faisal Baig came along as well, just to be sure that his friends were safe. After the helicopter lifted off from Zuudkhan, they used Greg's satellite phone to call home. From Tara and McCown's wife, Karen, they learned the details of the terrorist attacks that had destroyed the World Trade towers in New York City, damaged the Pentagon in Washington, D.C., and crashed a plane in a field in Pennsylvania. More than three thousand people had been killed.

Everyone was worried that Americans like Greg and McCown would now become targets of the terrorists who had attacked the United States. Tara was so relieved to hear from her husband that she burst into tears. "I know you're with your second family and they'll keep you safe," she shouted into the phone over the crackling static. "Finish your work and then come home to me, my love."

The helicopter took the Americans to a vacation spot, a fishing resort used by Pakistan's generals near Skardu. McCown wanted to get himself and his family out of Pakistan immediately, but the borders were shut down. No one was allowed in or out. Finally, Greg told him, "You're in the safest place on Earth right now. These people will protect you with their lives. Since we can't go anywhere, why don't we stick to the original program until we can put you on a plane?"

On Friday, September 14, Greg and McCown traveled to Kuardu, Changazi's village, as part of a crowd that was much larger than they had expected. Children had actually been going to the school in Kuardu for years. But Changazi wanted an official ceremony to inaugurate, or open it, with as many speeches and important people as possible. "It seemed like every politician, policeman, and military and religious leader in northern Pakistan came along to help inaugurate the Kuardu School," Greg said.

Syed Abbas gave the most important speech. "Today is

a day that you children will remember forever and tell your grandchildren," he said. "Today, from the darkness of illiteracy, the light of education shines bright.

"We share in the sorrow as people weep and suffer in America today as we inaugurate this school. Those who have committed this evil act against the innocent, the women and children, to create thousands of widows and orphans, do not do so in the name of Islam. By the grace of Allah the Almighty, may justice be served upon them.

"For this tragedy, I humbly ask Mr. George and Dr. Greg Sahib for their forgiveness. All of you, my brethren: Protect and embrace these two American brothers in our midst. Let no harm come to them. Share all you have to make their mission successful. . . ."

Syed Abbas paused, as if considering what to say next. Even the youngest children among the hundreds of people packed into the school's courtyard were silent.

"I request America to look into our hearts," he went on, "and see that the great majority of us are not terrorists, but good and simple people. Our land is stricken with poverty because we are without education. But today, another candle of knowledge has been lit. In the name of Allah the Almighty, may it light our way out of the darkness we find ourselves in."

"It was an incredible speech," Greg said. "And by the time Syed Abbas had finished, he had the entire crowd in tears. I wish all the Americans who think 'Muslim' is just another way of saying 'terrorist' could have been there that day. The true core **tenets** of Islam are justice, tolerance, and charity."

After the ceremony, many of the widows of Kuardu lined up to meet Greg and McCown. They pressed eggs into their hands, a traditional symbol of grief and mourning. They begged the two Americans to take the eggs to the women they thought of as sisters, the new widows far away in the village called New York.

The next day, Brigadier General Bashir himself flew McCown and his family in a helicopter to the airport, where they caught a plane home. "Thinking back on all of it," McCown said, "no one in Pakistan was anything but wonderful to us. I was so worried about what might happen to me. . . . But nothing did."

❦ ❦ ❦

Greg stayed in Pakistan and made his way to Korphe. During his many visits to Pakistan over the years, Greg always tried to stop by Korphe and visit with Haji Ali. As he walked over the swaying bridge, Greg realized that the high point where Haji Ali always stood to greet him was empty.

Twaha met Greg at the riverbank and gave him the news. His father had died a month ago.

The last fall, when Greg had come to visit Korphe, Sakina had been very ill. She'd died, refusing to leave Korphe to be taken to a hospital. Greg and Haji Ali had visited her grave. "I'm nothing without her," Haji Ali told his American son. "Nothing at all."

Then Haji Ali put his hand on Greg's shoulder, and at first Greg thought he was crying. But he was laughing.

"One day soon, you're going to come here looking for me and find me planted in the ground, too," Haji Ali said, chuckling.

Greg couldn't find anything funny in the idea of Haji Ali dying. He hugged the old man who'd already taught him so much and asked for one lesson more. "What should I do when that time comes?" he asked.

Haji Ali looked up at the summit of Korphe K2. "Listen to the wind," he said.

Now, with Twaha, Greg knelt by the grave of Korphe's old chief. Then he stood up, trying to imagine what Haji Ali would

Greg and Twaha in Korphe, at the grave of Haji Ali

David Oliver Relin

have said at such a moment. He remembered the old chief's words: "Listen to the wind."

Greg heard the wind whistling down the Braldu Gorge. It carried to him the sounds of Korphe's children, playing in the courtyard of the school. Here was Haji Ali's last lesson, he realized. "Think of them," he told himself. "Think only of them."

Faisal Baig had been right. Osama bin Laden had said that his organization, Al Qaeda, was responsible for the attacks on September 11. Afghanistan, where Al Qaeda was based, refused to allow foreign reporters to enter the country. The head of the Taliban government, Mullah Omar, had decided not to hand bin Laden over to the United States. War between the United States and Afghanistan, Pakistan's neighbor, seemed very likely.

The American **Embassy** had warned that Pakistan was no longer a safe place for Americans to visit. But Greg Mortenson wouldn't leave. He had work to do, visiting the CAI schools at refugee camps to see if they would be able to handle the many new students who would come once the fighting started.

While in Pakistan, Greg gave an interview to a reporter who had gone with him to visit the Afghan refugee schools. Greg asked Americans back home not to assume that all Muslims were guilty of terrorism. The families in the refugee camps, Greg said, weren't villains—they were victims. "These aren't the terrorists. These aren't the bad people," he said. He explained that the difference between becoming a good local citizen and a terrorist could be an education.

The warnings from the embassy got more and more serious. Eventually all Americans were ordered to leave Pakistan as war began in earnest between the United States and Afghanistan. Instead of leaving, Greg bought a plane ticket to Skardu, and flew back into a war zone. He spent the next month driving back and forth across northern Pakistan, checking on all the CAI projects, making sure everything was completed before the winter began. At the end of October, he finally got ready to head back to America.

His friend and bodyguard, Faisal Baig, drove him to the airport. Baig had dedicated himself to making sure Greg was safe anywhere he went in Pakistan. Now, as he said good-bye to his American friend, he had tears in his eyes.

"What is it, Faisal?" Greg asked, squeezing his shoulder.

"Now your country is at war," Baig said. "What can I do? How can I protect you there?"

🐦 🐦 🐦

Later, when Greg arrived home, he found out his interview with the reporter had been published by many newspapers across the country. For the first time in his life, Greg found himself opening hate mail from fellow Americans. Unsigned letters from around the country called Greg a "traitor" and wished pain upon him. "For the first time since starting my work in Pakistan, I thought about quitting," Greg says. "I expected something like this from an ignorant village mullah, but to get those kinds of letters from my fellow Americans made me wonder whether I should give up." But it was his wife, Tara, who encouraged Greg to go on.

"Now, more than ever, people in the United States need to hear about your message to promote peace and hope through education. Don't give up now." she said.

❦ ❦ ❦

But soon, Greg would find himself in danger again—this time he wouldn't be in Pakistan or the United States, but in Afghanistan.

A year before the terrorist attacks of September 11, Greg had visited Faisal Baig's village, near the border between Pakistan and Afghanistan. Standing with Baig, looking toward the border, he'd been startled to see a band of a dozen horsemen riding toward him. "They jumped off their horses and came straight at me," he said. "They were the wildest-looking men 'd ever seen." He remembered the time he'd been kidnapped in Waziristan in 1996, and thought, Uh-oh! Here we go again.

The leader, a man with a rifle slung over his shoulder, strode toward Greg. Baig stepped into his path. Then, a moment later, the two men were hugging and talking excitedly.

"My friend," Baig told Greg. "He looks for you many times."

Baig's friend, a village chief, was a **nomad** of the Kirghiz tribe. He and his men had ridden for six days to find Greg.

"For me hard life is no problem," he said as Baig translated his words for Greg. "But for children no good. We have not much food, not much house, and no school. We know about Dr. Greg build school in Pakistan. So you can come build for us? We give land, stone, men, everything. Come now and stay with us for the winter so we can have good discuss and make a school?"

Greg explained that he had to go home in a few days. And that he'd need the approval of the CAI board for a new project. But he swore to himself that he'd find a way to help these Afghans. He laid his hand on the man's shoulder. "Tell him I need go home now. Tell him working in Afghanistan is very difficult for me," he told Baig. "But I promise I come visit his family as soon as I can. Then we discuss if building some school is possible."

The man smiled and laid his own hand on Greg's shoulder. Then he and his men returned to Afghanistan to report back to *Commandhan* Abdul Rashid Khan, the **warlord** who controlled their part of Afghanistan.

Now, in the winter of 2002, more than a year after the attacks of September 11, Greg thought he might be able to start keeping his promise to those Afghan horsemen. American soldiers, fighting alongside Afghan troops known as the Northern Alliance, had driven the Taliban from power. Greg understanding that the Taliban had supported and protected Osama bin Laden and his Al Qaeda terrorist group, had approved of the war at first. But he became more and mor

Greg with supporters and members of CAI's staff in Skardu
Front row, kneeling: Saidullah Baig, Sarfraz Khan. Back row, standing (left to right): Mohammed Nazir, Faisal Baig, Ghulam Parvi, Greg Mortenson, Apo Razak, Mehdi Ali, Suleman Minhas

upset as he heard how many civilians, ordinary people who were not soldiers, were dying as American planes dropped bombs. Some of the dead, Greg was sure, must be children.

He heard from staff members how children in the Afghan refugee camps often picked up the bright yellow pods of unexploded cluster bombs because they looked like the yellow packets of food that American planes dropped. He worried about the students who'd studied at CAI schools in the refugee camps in Pakistan. Some had returned with their families to Afghanistan before this new fighting. At night, he remembered their faces and wondered if they were still alive.

There was still fighting in some areas of Afghanistan, but

Greg decided that the capital, Kabul, which was in the hands of the American forces, was probably safe enough for him to visit. Once his plane landed in Kabul, he wasn't so sure. He could see pieces of bombed planes lying by the runway. At his hotel, which had no electricity or running water, Greg could hear guns firing and rockets landing outside.

With the help of his taxi driver, Abdullah Rahman, and a friend of his, Greg drove around Kabul to see schools and figure out what kind of help might be needed. The schools had been badly damaged in the war, but were supposed to reopen later that spring. But only a few of Kabul's 159 schools were able to hold classes. And even these that were still standing had to take groups of students in shifts, one after the other, sometimes holding classes outside or in buildings that were more piles of rubble than anything else.

At the Durkhani High School, Greg met the principal, Uzra Faizad. She told Greg that the number of students who wanted to go to her school grew every day. Under the Taliban, girls had been forbidden to go to school. Now, with the Taliban gone, they were trying to get the education that had been kept from them.

"I was just overwhelmed listening to Uzra's story," Greg said. "Here was this strong, proud woman trying to do the impossible. Her school's boundary wall had been blown to rubble. The roof had fallen in. Still, she was coming to work every day and putting the place back together because she was passionate about education being the only way to solve Afghanistan's problems."

Greg decided to return to Pakistan, gather up some school supplies, and come back to Kabul to start helping out in any way he could. Julia Bergman, who worked on the CAI's board, came with him. The trip to Kabul took eleven hours.

"I was surprised to see that the whole border area was wide open," Greg says.

"All along the road we saw burned-out, bombed tanks and other military vehicles," says Bergman.

Greg and Bergman toured the schools in Kabul and nearby towns, trying to help where they could. At one middle school, they saw classes being held inside huge metal shipping containers and a rusty tank. The girls had no shelter at all. "Eighty girls were forced to study outside," Greg said. "They were trying to hold class, but the wind kept whipping sand in their eyes and tipping over their blackboard." Greg unloaded notebooks and pencils from Abdullah's taxi. The girls were thrilled and clutched the notebooks tightly to keep them from blowing away.

As Greg walked back toward the taxi, four U.S Army helicopters dipped down from the sky to fly overhead at high speed. The students at the school were terrified. The girls' blackboard blew over in the wind created by the helicopters and shattered against the stony ground.

The next day, Greg and Bergman went to deliver supplies to Uzra Faizad's school. They saw that her students had to climb up ladders built of logs to get into classrooms on the second floor, because the stairs had been blown away. But even so, the school was teaching three shifts of students every day. Uzra was

Three Cups of Tea

delighted to see them and invited them into her home—a one-room shed on the school's property.

During the time of the Taliban, Uzra had taught girls secretly. Now that the Taliban had gone, she talked openly about how important it was for girls to get an education. She served her guests tea, apologizing that she had no sugar to go with it. "There is one favor I must ask you," Uzra said after everyone had tasted their tea. "We're very grateful that the Americans chased out the Taliban. But for five months now, I haven't received my salary, even though I was told to expect it soon. Can you discuss my problem with someone in America to see if they know what happened?"

Greg gave Uzra forty dollars and another twenty for each of her teachers. On the plane back home, he could not stop thinking about her. "I was so upset I paced the aisles of the planes all the way to Washington, D.C.," he said. "If we couldn't do something as simple as seeing that a hero like Uzra gets her forty-dollar-a-month salary, then how could we ever hope to do the hard work it takes to win the war on terror?"

❦ ❦ ❦

When he was not traveling in Afghanistan and Pakistan, Greg spent much of his time giving speeches, telling people about the CAI and its work and the lives of the poor in Pakistan and Afghanistan. Sometimes he spoke to large crowds, sometimes to small groups. Once, before his trip to Kabul with Bergman, he met six people in a basement room in Montana and told them about himself, the CAI, and the mistakes he believed the U.S

136

government was making in the way it was fighting the war in Afghanistan.

After his speech, one of his listeners introduced herself. "I'm Mary Bono," she said. "Actually Representative Mary Bono." She was a member of the U.S. **House of Representatives**. "I have to tell you I've learned more from you in the last hour than I have in all the **briefings** I've been to on Capitol Hill since September 11," she went on. "We've got to get you up there." She handed him her business card with her telephone number on it and told him to call her to schedule a speech in Washington.

When he arrived back in the United States after his trip to Kabul, Greg did just that. With his mind on everything he'd just seen in Afghanistan, he landed in Washington, D.C. "When I arrived, I had no idea what to do. I felt like I had been dropped in a remote Afghan village where I didn't know the customs," Greg said. "Mary spent an entire day with me, showing me how everything worked. . . . She started introducing me around, saying, 'Here's someone you need to meet. This is Greg Mortenson.'" He was embarrassed when she told people, "He's a real American hero."

Bono had arranged for Greg to give a lecture and invited every member of Congress to come. "After I heard Greg speak, it was the least I could do," Bono says. "I meet so many people day in and day out who say they're trying to do good and help people. But Greg is the real thing. . . . And I'm his biggest fan. The sacrifices that he and his family have made are staggering. He represents the best of America."

After setting up his old slide projector, still held togethe with duct tape, Greg turned to face the room full of people He spoke about Uzra and her missing salary and about how important it was that America keep its promise to rebuilc Afghanistan.

One congressman interrupted him. "Building schools for kids is just fine and dandy," he said. "But our primary need as a nation now is security. Without security, what does all this matter?"

Greg took a breath. He felt his anger flare. But he tried to speak calmly. "I don't do what I'm doing to fight terror," he said. "I do it because I care about kids. . . . But working over there, I've learned a few things. I've learned that terror doesn't happen because some group of people somewhere like Pakistar or Afghanistan simply decide to hate us. It happens because children aren't being offered a bright enough future that they had a reason to choose life over death."

Greg hoped he'd said enough to convince some of the people in the room that the danger to America from terrorists like Al Qaeda would go away only when the children of countries like Afghanistan and Pakistan could get an education that would lift them out of poverty. With a chance at a better life, they would not be easy prey for terrorists who taught them to hate countries like the United States. Better schools in Afghanistar and Pakistan would leave the United States more secure, Greg thought. He hoped the politicians in the room believed him.

In 2002, Greg was back in Korphe, and this time he'd brought along a reporter named Kevin Fedarko. Fedarko was reporting on the fighting between India and Pakistan, and he'd asked for Greg's assistance. "Greg bent over backward to help me. . . . I had no connections in Pakistan and never could have done it myself," Fedarko said.

On their first day in Korphe, Fedarko watched as Greg and the elders of the village had a meeting. "There was always a lot to work out," Greg said. "I had to get reports about the school, find out if anything needed fixing, if the students needed supplies, if the teachers were getting their pay regularly." It was business as usual, with everybody talking, laughing, shouting, and arguing, when something happened that was not usual at all.

A young woman walked into the room and took a seat in front of Greg. She spoke up, interrupting the men who were talking all around her.

"Dr. Greg," she said in Balti. "You made our village a promise once, and you fulfilled it when you built our school. But you made me another promise the day the school was completed. Do you remember it?"

Whenever Greg visited one of CAI's schools, he made it a point to shake every student's hand, and ask each one what he or she wanted to be one day. He remembered this girl well. The young woman was Jahan, Twaha's daughter and Haji Ali's granddaughter. And the promise Greg had made to her was one he made to all the students in the CAI schools—that if they studied hard, he would help them reach whatever goals they set for themselves. Jahan had been one of Korphe's best students. Greg had often listened to her talk about her hopes for a career.

"I told you my dream was to be a doctor one day, and you said you would help," Jahan told Greg. "Well, that day is here. You must keep your promise to me. I'm ready to begin my medical training, and I need twenty thousand rupees."

Jahan unfolded a piece of paper and gave it to Greg. On it she'd written, in English, a description of the school she wanted to attend in Skardu, the courses she would take, and how much it would cost.

"This is great, Jahan," said Greg. "I'll read it when I have time and discuss it with your father."

"No!" Jahan exclaimed, in English. Then she switched back to Balti. "You don't understand. My class starts next week. I need money now!"

Jahan, the Braldu Valley's first educated woman

Greg grinned. He was delighted to see that Jahan had learned one of the lessons he hoped all the girls at the CAI schools would learn—how to stand up for herself. From a child's pink backpack full of CAI money, he counted out twenty thousand rupees—about four hundred dollars—and handed it to Jahan's father for her tuition.

Kevin Fedarko, the reporter, had been watching in amazement.

"It was one of the most incredible things I'd ever seen in my life," he said. "Here comes this teenage girl, in the center of a very conservative Islamic village, waltzing into a circle of men, breaking through about sixteen layers of tradition at once. She had graduated from school and was the first educated woman in a valley of about six hundred people. She didn't defer to anyone, sat down right in front of Greg, and handed him . . . a proposal, in English, to better herself and improve the life of her village. . . . I told Greg, 'What you're doing here is a much more important story than the one I've come to report. I have to find some way to tell it.'"

Later that fall, in New York City, Fedarko had lunch with an old friend who was the editor of *Parade* magazine, and told him all about the CAI's work. The editor called Greg. In the spring of 2003, just as the United States' war against Iraq began, 34 million copies of the magazine went out to readers with Greg Mortenson's picture on the cover. Inside, Fedarko told the story of Jahan's bold plans for her education and of Greg Mortenson's work. "If we truly want a **legacy** of peace for our children," Greg aid in the article, "we need to understand that this is a war that will ultimately be won with books, not with bombs."

In one day, that article reached more people than Greg could have reached with months of speeches. Letters and e-mails poured in from all over the United States and from twenty foreign countries. A few days after the story appeared, Greg went to the post office for his mail. There was a note in his post office box telling him to pick up his letters at the counter. "So you're Greg Mortenson," the postmaster said. "I hope you brought a wheelbarrow." Greg loaded five sacks of mail into his car. He came back the next day for four more. "I felt like America had spoken. My tribe had spoken," Greg said. "And the amazing thing was, there was only one negative letter in the whole bunch."

Greg went on to say, "What really humbled me was how the response came from all sorts of people, from church groups, Muslims, Hindus, and Jews." And many of the letters came with donations. Jake, a thirteen-year-old from Philadelphia, sent a thousand dollars of his bar mitzvah money. A captain in the U.S. Army wrote that the CAI was now his favorite charity. Gradually the CAI had more than a million dollars in the bank. Greg wanted to get right back to Pakistan and Afghanistan and put the money to work, but he agreed to a few things that the board wanted: a real office for the CAI, some staff to work there, and, at long last, a raise for himself.

Greg was also able to give raises to the people who worked for him in Pakistan. And he had a new idea. "For a long time,

I've been worrying about what to do when our student graduate," he said during his next trip to Pakistan. "Mr. Parvi would you look into what it would cost to build a **hostel** in Skardu so our best students would have someplace to stay if we give them scholarships to continue their education?"

"I'd be delighted, Dr. Sahib," said Parvi, smiling.

"Oh, and one more thing," Greg said.

"Yes, Dr. Greg, sir."

"Yasmine would be a perfect candidate to receive one of the CAI's first scholarships. Can you let me know what her tuition would be if she went to private high school in the fall?"

Yasmine was Parvi's fifteen-year-old daughter. For a rare moment, the normally talkative Ghulam Parvi was struck dumb, his mouth hanging open. "I don't know what to say," he said.

"*Allah-u-Akbhar!*" another CAI worker shouted as everybody at the meeting exploded into laughter.

🌱 🌱 🌱

In the fall of 2003, the same year the article appeared in *Parade*, Greg returned to Skardu. There, he met Jahan and her classmate Tahira, who had come to Skardu together to go to high school, both with scholarships from the CAI. On his last day in town, Greg stopped by with Jahan's father, Twaha, to see how the girls were doing in the apartment they shared. Jahan proudly served him tea, as her grandmother Sakina had done so often.

Tahira told Greg that, once she graduated, she planned to return to Korphe to teach along with her father, Hussein. When she and Jahan went upside, or back into the mountains to Korphe, she saw a difference in how people treated her. "I've had this chance," she said. "Now when we go upside, all the people look at us, our clothes, and think we are fashionable ladies. I think every girl of the Braldu deserves the chance to come downside at least once. Then their life will change. I think the greatest service I can perform is to go back and ensure that this happens for all of them."

Jahan refilled Greg's teacup. "Before I met you, Dr. Greg, I had no idea what education was," she said. "But now I think it is like water. It is important for everything in life."

"What about marriage?" Greg asked. He knew that, once Jahan got married, a Balti husband might not support her goals to educate herself.

"Don't worry, Dr. Greg," Twaha said, laughing. "This girl has learned your lesson too well. She has already made it clear she must finish her studies before we can even discuss marrying her to a suitable boy. And I agree. I will sell all my land if necessary so she can complete her education. I owe that to the memory of my father."

"So what will you do?" Greg asked Jahan.

"You won't laugh?" she said.

"I might," Greg teased.

Jahan took a breath. "When I was a little girl and I would see a gentleman or a lady with good, clean clothes, I would run away and hide my face. But after I graduated from the Korphe School, I felt a big change in my life. I felt I was clear and clean and could go before anybody and discuss anything.

"And now that I am already in Skardu, I feel that anything is possible. I don't want to be just a health worker. I want to be such a woman that I can start a hospital . . . and look over all the health problems of all the women in the Braldu. I want to become a very famous woman of this area," Jahan went on, twirling the hem of her headscarf around her finger. "I want to be a 'Superlady,'" she said, grinning as if daring anybody to tell her that she couldn't.

Greg didn't laugh. He imagined how proud Haji Ali would have felt if he'd lived long enough to see this day.

The king sat in the window seat.

Greg recognized Zahir Shah, the king of Afghanistan, from pictures on old Afghan money. The king and Greg were both on a flight to Kabul, the capital of Afghanistan. When Shah looked away from the window, he met Greg's eyes.

"*As-salaam alaikum*, sir," Greg said.

"And to you, sir," Shah replied. "American?"

"Yes, sir," Greg said.

"Are you a journalist?" the king asked.

"No, sir," Greg said. "I build schools, for girls."

"And what is your business in my country, if I may ask?"

"I begin construction of five or six schools in the spring, *Inshallah*," Greg explained. "I'm coming to deliver the money to get them going." Greg explained that his schools would not be in Kabul, the capital, but in the Wakhan, the distant area near the border with Pakistan. The king was surprised. Greg told him the story of the Afghan horseman who'd ridden over into Pakistan and asked him to bring schools to their villages. "I promised them I'd come . . . discuss schools with them, but I haven't been able to get there until now," he said.

"We don't see many Americans in Afghanistan anymore," the king said. "A year ago this plane would have been full of journalists and aid workers. But now they are all in Iraq. America has forgotten us." Then he placed his hand on Greg's. "I'm glad one American is here at least," he said. "The man you want to see up north is *Commandhan* Sardhar Khan." The king gave Greg his business card, and on the back of it he printed his thumbprint in black ink. It might be helpful, he said, if Greg showed the card to Khan. "Allah be with you," he added. "And go with my blessing."

❦ ❦ ❦

Greg wanted to go from Kabul to Faizabad, the largest city in northeastern Afghanistan. He knew it would be a dangerous two-day trip through the countryside. But he didn't feel that he had a choice. He was determined to keep his promise to the Kirghiz horseman. While he had been gone, they had traveled six days each way to deliver a message to Faisal Baig. There were more than five thousand students in their area and no schools at all. They were waiting, *Inshallah*, for Greg to come and build them.

Greg sent his friend Abdullah out to rent a car or truck that could travel over the rough countryside. At midnight, he was awakened by a loud knocking on the door of his hotel room.

Abdullah had good news. He'd rented a jeep and found a young man named Kais who would come along and translate. He also had bad news. They would have to cross the mountains by traveling through the Salang Tunnel, and that tunnel would close the next morning at six A.M.

"When will it open again?" Greg asked.

Abdullah shrugged. "Twelve hours? Two days? Who can know?"

Greg began to repack his suitcases.

Before they reached the Salang Tunnel, Greg fell asleep in the car. He woke when the jeep stopped, in perfect darkness. They were inside the tunnel, and the jeep's radiator had quit working. The car was stuck, and in the worst possible place in the tunnel. Greg and Abdullah peered under the hood, trying to figure out if they could fix the problem, when a truck roared downhill toward them. The driver could not see the jeep until he was almost upon it. At the last moment, he swerved, ripping off the jeep's sideview mirror as he drove by.

"Let's go!" Greg yelled. The three ran along the tunnel's wall and found a doorway to the outside. But the moment Greg looked at the ground, he stopped. He'd spotted a stone that was painted red. Then another. And another.

There are millions of **land mines** buried all over Afghanistan, left there by armies after years and years of war. When one is found—usually because it explodes—rocks in the area are painted red, as a warning. Even though children are taught about land mines in school, hundreds still die every year from stepping on them. Greg knew that they did not dare try to keep walking. The tunnel was dangerous, but not half as dangerous as walking through land mines. They ducked back inside.

"I don't know what would have happened if the next vehicle wasn't a truck, climbing slowly uphill," Greg said. "But thank God it was. I jumped out in front of it and flagged it down."

There were five men in the truck, smugglers with a load of stolen refrigerators. But they let Greg and Kais ride in the truck's cab, shared a bunch of grapes with them, and the truck pushed their jeep, with Abdullah steering it, uphill. When they reached the top of the hill, still inside the tunnel, Abdullah, Greg, and Kais climbed back into their jeep. They coasted down the hill and out into the daylight.

"I was so happy to get out of that tunnel and into the light that I hugged Abdullah so hard I almost made him crash the jeep," Greg said. They managed to repair the radiator with a piece cut from the spare tire and some duct tape from Greg's backpack, and were back on their way.

They continued on until evening, when suddenly a burst of machine-gun fire from up ahead made Abdullah slam on the brakes. He backed the jeep up quickly, but more gunshots came from behind. "Come!" Abdullah ordered, pulling Greg and Kais out of the jeep and into a muddy ditch, where they lay facedown, hoping to keep out of the way of bullets. They'd found themselves in the middle of a battle between two gangs of opium smugglers.

"They fired back and forth at each other over our heads,

Greg said. "I stopped thinking about escape and started thinking about my kids, trying to imagine how Tara would explain the way I'd died to them, and wondering if they would understand what I was trying to do—how I didn't mean to leave them, that I was trying to help kids like them over here. I decided Tara would make them understand. And that was a pretty good feeling."

Then headlights appeared from an approaching truck, and the gunfire died down. Abdullah jumped out of the ditch to wave the truck down, and called to Kais to translate as he asked for a ride for the foreigner, Greg.

Abdullah called for Greg to come. Greg ran from the ditch and jumped in the back of the truck, which was filled with goat hides. Abdullah threw a goat hide over him to hide him from view.

"What about you and the boy?" Greg asked.

"Allah will watch over us," said Abdullah. The smugglers were shooting at each other, not at them. "We wait, then take the jeep back to Kabul," Abdullah said, and he slapped the back of the truck with his hand. It jolted away along the highway.

Under a pile of rotting goatskins, Greg covered his nose with his hand and watched the gunfire resume, hoping Abdullah was right. He was. Kais and Abdullah would make it safely back to Kabul. But Greg wouldn't learn that until the following week.

As the truck rolled on, Greg realized that he was going to have to go without dinner. He had a bag of peanuts in his backpack—but his backpack, he remembered, was still in the jeep. In it, along with the peanuts, was the king's business card with his thumbprint on the back. He felt the pockets of his vest, and luckily he still had his passport and some American money.

"I was alone," Greg said later. "I was covered in mud and goat blood. I'd lost my luggage. I didn't speak the local language. I hadn't had a meal for days, but I felt surprisingly good. I felt like I had all those years earlier, riding . . . up the Indus Gorge with my supplies for the Korphe School, having no clue what was ahead of me. My plan for the next few days was vague. And I had no idea if I'd succeed. But you know what? It wasn't a bad feeling at all."

The truck dropped Greg off in Faizabad. He slept in the hallway of a hotel. The next morning he found a father and son who agreed to drive him in another jeep to Sardhar Khan's headquarters in the city of Baharak.

Khan was a *commandhan*, a man who ruled the province of **Badakhshan** as if he were its king. He was known as a smart and ruthless fighter, and he had his own militia, soldiers who were his private army. He could be harsh and cruel to his enemies. But he also took care of the people of Badakhshan who were loyal to him. Greg knew that he needed Khan on his side if he wanted to build schools in this area.

It took three hours to reach Baharak, as the jeep crept along ledges above a river that wound through a rocky canyon. Finally they drove into the marketplace of the town. The only other car there was a white jeep. Greg waved it down. He figured that anyone who could afford such a good jeep would know where to find Sardhar Khan.

The driver, a man with piercing black eyes and a neatly trimmed beard, got out to talk to Greg.

"I'm looking for Sardhar Khan," Greg said in **Dari**, the local language. He'd gotten Kais to teach him a few words on the drive from Kabul.

"He is here," the man said in English.

"Where?"

"I am he. I am *Commandhan* Khan."

❦ ❦ ❦

It was Friday, the Muslim holy day. Greg waited nervously on the roof of Sardhar Khan's compound as the *commandhan* went to the mosque to pray with the other village men. On the rooftops of buildings nearby, men with guns kept on eye on the American's movements.

To the southeast, Greg could see the snowy peaks of Pakistan's mountains. He knew that Faisal Baig's village of Zuudkhan was not far. In his mind, he drew lines that ran from Baig to the schools he'd built and the villages he'd spent so much time in, connecting people and places he knew and loved to this lonely rooftop. He told himself that he was not alone.

Then Khan returned from his prayers. "And what has an American come so far from Kabul to talk about?" he asked.

Greg told the warlord his story. He explained how the Kirghiz horsemen had ridden into Pakistan to find him and ask for his help. He told of his trip from Kabul, the gunfight by the roadside, his escape under the goatskins.

Then the fearsome Afghan warlord did something astonishing. He shouted with joy and wrapped Greg in a huge hug.

"Yes! Yes! You're Dr. Greg!" he exclaimed. One of his men, Abdul Rashid, had told him all about Greg. "This is incredible," Khan said, pacing with excitement. "And to think. I didn't even arrange a meal or a welcome from the village elders. Forgive me."

Khan ordered a feast to be prepared for his American guest

Greg with Sardhar Khan

Then he and Greg walked in circles on the roof, discussing where to build schools.

Khan knew all there was to know about the places where Greg was eager to begin work. Quickly he listed five villages that needed schools. And he told Greg about all the girls in the area who had nowhere to study. In Faizabad alone, he said, five thousand teenage girls were trying to hold classes in the fields outside the boys' high school.

As the sun started to set behind the **Pamir Mountains** to the west, Khan put one hand on Greg's back and pointed with the other. "Look here, look at these hills," he went on. "There has been far too much dying in those hills." Each stone in the mountains, Khan said, stood for a martyr, someone who'd died in battle. "Now we must make their sacrifice worthwhile," he finished, turning to Greg. "We must turn those stones into schools."

In that moment, Greg Mortenson saw what the rest of his life would be like. There would be new languages and new customs to learn. He would spend months apart from his family. There would be dangers he couldn't yet imagine.

Greg put his hands on Sardhar Khan's shoulders, just as he had done to Haji Ali, so many years ago. Once, long ago, he'd decided to climb the second-highest mountain in the world in his sister's honor. Now, looking into the eyes of an Afghan warlord, he dedicated himself to climbing an even higher mountain—to keep bringing education, and hope, and chances of a better life to the children of Afghanistan and Pakistan.

Christa would have been proud.

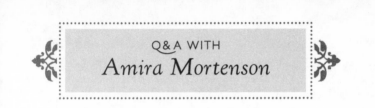

## Tell us a little bit about yourself and your family.

Hi. My name is Amira Eliana Mortenson. Amira means female leader in the Persian language, and Eliana means "Gift of God" in the Chagga language of Tanzania, Africa. I'm twelve years old, and in seventh grade, and my favorite classes are music and Spanish. My dad is Greg Mortenson, and my mom is Tara Bishop. My brother Khyber is eight, and in third grade.

We live in Montana in the same house both Khyber and I were born in, instead of a hospital. Three hours after Khyber

Khyber, Tara, and Amira; 2008

Lila Bishop

was born, I took him to my preschool for show-and-tell.

We have an old dog named Tashi, and a guinea pig.

Three of my favorite things are singing, theater, and martial arts. My voice teacher, Jeni Fleming, is a professional singer, and we like singing jazz together. At home I always listen to hit songs, gospel, and jazz. I also love to sing Broadway show tunes, and I sing really loud when I am in the shower.

My closet has a huge dress-up box that we use for costumes and homemade plays. My friends and I get creative and pretend we're different characters and people. Since I was five, I've been in a summer theater camp called Equinox. Acting and improv is fun, and I like that it's a great way to learn how to be creative. I also like to play, goof off, and have sleepovers with my friends.

Tae kwon do is totally my favorite sport. It is a martial art form started in Korea. I got my black belt in 2008, and became a Montana state champion. I'm a junior instructor for younger kids. In tae kwon do we learn about self-defense, but we also learn to have respect, discipline, loyalty, and honor. I've been doing it about three years.

### Tell me about your song, "Three Cups of Tea."

It's a song that I recorded with Jeni Fleming in Nashville, Tennessee. Jeni's husband, Jake, did the lyrics with phrases and words I helped to write. It was cool to record with professional musicians. We sell the CD online, and it helps raise money to buy supplies for kids halfway around the world who are eager to go to school.

Tara Bishop

Amira gets her black belt; 2008

### Tell me about some of the lyrics.

The song starts with the Arabic words *As-salaam alaikum*, which means "Peace be with you." It goes on to my favorite part, "If I give a penny for a pencil / my hero writes a word. / Her words become great tools / his stories make wise the fools. / I believe it's three cups away." What that means is that even with a penny a kid can make a difference and give other children power and hope.

Women who have an education will also help encourage their kids to go to school and be good citizens, and not be violent, kill people, or go to war at a young age. It's hard to believe the world is so lame, and can't help the over 100 million kids who can't go to school because of slavery, poverty, or discrimination. Many kids are forced to work twelve hours every day to make fireworks, carpets, soccer balls, or to work on farms. That really bothers me. Every child should have the right to go to school. Without education, nothing's possible, really.

In Pakistan and Afghanistan, a penny can buy a pencil. When a kid learns to read and write, they feel more connected to the outside world, and have better opportunities in life. When they write they have hope, and when they have hope they can accomplish anything. My dad always tells us that anyone can make a difference, and we should not be afraid to follow our dreams. Education teaches girls to be strong and wonderful women. It's a great thing.

### Have you been to Pakistan or Afghanistan?

I've been to Pakistan a few times, but never Afghanistan. My first trip to Pakistan was when I was eight months old as a baby, and the most recent trip was in 2007 with my brother, Khyber.

### How do you get around?

We mostly travel in a jeep and truck, or walk. But also we

Amira (age 3) in Kalash tribal clothes; 1999

also go in planes, buses, helicopters, bicycles, wheelbarrows, and sometimes on a donkey.

### What's it like to travel in Pakistan?

I love being there. It's totally different. The last time I went was in the summer of 2007 when I was ten. We visited schools and friends' homes.

### Do you have any friends in Pakistan?

One of my best friends is Hussein. He was my dad's jeep driver for many years until he had a stroke. He has six kids, and shares his house with his parents and elders. In the United States, we mostly live with only our family. But in Pakistan and Afghanistan, most people also live with their relatives or parents and have a lot of respect for old people. It's a great way to grow up.

### What was Hussein's house like?

It's a mud-brick house with two levels. There are seven rooms, a kitchen, and a courtyard with a hand-pump water well. There's no furniture, but comfortable carpets everywhere. You sit, eat, and sleep on the floor. There's a ladder to the flat roof, where there's a whole bunch of corn, apricots, and cherries drying in the sun. Next to the house, there is a shed where cows and goats are kept, and used for milk, yogurt, and cheese. It's really neat.

## *What are the schools like? What do they look like?*

They're small, and usually square, and comfortable. The school floors are dirt, which is warmer than cement floors. They have white-washed walls, with red bucket flower pots along the stairs. On the inside, they have a chalkboard and some small desks. Usually there will be two or three classes outside and about four or five classes inside. The students share desks and supplies. Kids are hardly ever selfish, and share everything since they are so poor. I've never heard a kid whine over there, if you can imagine that! The kids are proud to go to school in a building, instead of sitting outside.

Rondu School, Dassu Valley

Greg Mortenson

# Three Cups of Tea

*How are they different from the school that you go to?*

The schools are not as modern as in the United States, but they're nice and the kids learn a lot. In the States, we think bigger is better. But if you aren't learning, it doesn't matter. I could see myself going to a school like that. My small school in Montana is cool, because it has couches with pillows, tables, and posters on the wall, and we also have computers, art supplies, science materials, and music. But again, the best thing are our teachers, who really care. When you go to their schools in Pakistan, they have a chalkboard, desks, notebooks, and textbooks.

*Do you wear a uniform at your school?*

No, I don't. But in Pakistan and Afghanistan they wear uniforms. They wear a *shalwar kamiz*, which is like pajamas, with a green, blue, or black top, with a white-pants bottom. When I was there, I wore the traditional school uniform, too. The girls wear a **dupatta**, which is a scarf that goes on your head, so I wore one, too. It shows respect for women to cover their bodies and hair. I didn't want the kids to feel like I was more important than them, because I'm not. I'm just a kid. They respected me—an American girl who wears their kind of clothes. It definitely felt important to me. Showing up in skimpy shorts and a tank top is kinda inappropriate and disrespectful.

*What was your favorite thing about visiting Pakistan?*

Seeing the joy on kids' faces was probably my favorite

thing—to see them happy to be in school, and get new supplies. You can feel and hear the hope they have—hearing the hope that anyone can give them by saying, "If you try hard enough, you will become what you want to be."

It was also wonderful to be with my family for twenty-four hours a day for weeks, and do everything together. In the United States, everybody is so busy with work, activities, and chores; we don't realize that the best thing in life is to be with your family.

I also spent a lot of time with friends like Jahan, who is in *Three Cups of Tea*. We sketched portraits of each other, and she loved my Mini Groovy Girls.

Tahera, Chocho, and Jahan

Greg Mortenson

*A couple of places you sang. How was that?*

It was hard, because I get worried if I sing something disrespectful or wrong, and I'm going to disappoint these girls. But they really enjoyed it, and they love to sing, too.

*Were you scared to travel?*

Nope, not really, but we do have to be careful sometimes. On Friday, which is called Juma, we don't go out, and usually hang out with family and friends at home because on some Friday afternoons there are riots, and bombings.

*Tell me about something that riled you up when you visited a school.*

When a school has a ceremony, the important men and guests sit around and are boring. They sit, talk, and eat food that could last them a week, maybe. I was at one of the ceremonies and I saw that the important women sat in a little room with less food. And the kids got very little to eat. About ten girls shared a small plate of rice with the tiniest bit of meat sauce. They ate with their hands, and that's all they got. And even the poorest girls offered me food; they wanted to share. It's heartbreaking when they treat women and girls so lowly, and it's hard to eat when you are with starving kids. I felt like I was being so spoiled.

*What did you eat when you were there?*

When we stay at the Indus Hotel in Skardu, we eat porridge for breakfast with toast, and for dinner it's usually rice or potatoes, some vegetables with a little bit of chicken. Some people try to please us and make American food like french fries, but I prefer local food. For lunch, we usually ate ramen noodles, or something simple. We didn't actually eat a whole lot. Here, it's like we live to eat, and there it's like they eat to live.

## What sort of food are the students at the Central Asia Institute schools eating at home?

They get mostly *chapattis*, which is like pita bread, or rice, and rarely meat. They're so skinny. It's like, we Americans have too much food, and then you go over there and they hardly have any.

I got my dad to start a lunch program in some of the schools,

Hushe schoolgirls

Jimmy Chen

and I hope it makes it to all the schools. Even a *chapatti* with warm milk tea in their bellies would help kids stay alert and strong. I've drawn a design of big colorful bowls that kids can share and eat together, which they are used to. Most of the schools have clean drinking water, which is so important. Millions of kids die around the world because they get sick from bad water. We never think of that when we use a faucet.

### What surprised you most?

There are animals everywhere. Chickens, cows, goats, sheep, horses, yaks, and everything. It's like an animal farm

Amira with schoolgirls; 2007

even in the city. Horses and cows share the road with cars and bicycles. When's the last time you saw a chicken and horse running down Main Street?

Also, Pakistan is so different compared to the United States, but it's also really similar, too. It's weird to think how something can be so close to you, but so totally different.

### You took a lot of photos on your trips. What is your favorite?

My favorite photo is the photo of me in the sea of girls in their blue uniforms and their white *shalwar kamiz*, and I'm reading a Dr. Seuss book with them. We're hunched together, and I'm reading with like a thousand girls around. That's total girl power and cool energy.

### What is it like having your dad gone so much of the time because of his work?

That is a really hard question. I don't like it. I really don't like it.

### What don't you like about it?

Just that I feel like the public gets more time with him than we do. People treat my dad like a rock star, or chase him because they think he's really famous—but to me, he's just a normal dad and guy, you know? And what most people don't know is that my dad is shy and not a socializer like me. He has to push himself to meet thousands of people every month. It's hard when I see friends playing catch with their dads, or just see their dads hugging them, or giving them compliments—and then knowing that my dad is in a really difficult and dangerous place, and that he might not come back.

*Do you think you could relate to kids who either don't have a mom or dad, or their mom or dad has a dangerous job or is in the military?*

Yeah, definitely. I feel really close to those kids. I think it's really hard for kids like us, because you want your parents and nothing can replace them. It's hard when they're not there. And people should know what a big sacrifice it is for kids whose parents are gone a lot, because they are making the world a better place. You know, there are thousands of kids in the United States whose parents are gone a lot, especially those who have dads or moms in the military in Iraq or Afghanistan. My heart goes out to them. And we should try to always support them. I write letters to kids whose parents are serving in Iraq or Afghanistan, to tell them to hang in there, it's not easy, but we care about them. It means a lot when someone just comes up to me and says, "Thanks for sharing your dad" or "I understand."

Like, most kids who have parents gone or on dangerous jobs, they don't get to share in special time. The parents don't get to teach kids how to tie their shoes, read a book, ride a bike, or how to swim. Their parents don't get to go to every single birthday party or every music concert. When I work really hard for something, I want my supporters to be there, and my dad is one of my biggest supporters. So when I look out in the audience and I don't see him out there, it makes me depressed. But I think it helps knowing that you're not the only person whose parents are gone. We should all kind of help each other out and say, "Are you okay?"

## You travel with your dad a fair amount, just you and him together. What's that like?

It's hard. I mean, everyone wants to talk or be with him, and he always takes time for everyone. Even though when we travel together, I sometimes feel like I'm not with him, you know? What's great though is that we are close, and he is like one of my best buddies.

## He's at work. Are you at work, too?

Yes. It's hard, though. At least once a month I sing or speak at one of my dad's lectures. I like speaking to kids, 'cause they're easy to talk to. My favorite part is hearing what they have to say, because so many kids don't know about poverty or illiteracy. I think it's a good idea to influence kids about sharing and caring; then when they get older they can help other people in poor countries. Peace is more powerful than war, and kids need to know that also.

I really like to tell kids about **Pennies for Peace**™ (www. penniesforpeace.org), a program my dad started a long time ago. The program gets kids here in the United States inspired to collect pennies to raise money for causes, and learn about other cultures and philanthropy. It encourages kids to pick what they want to support with the pennies they gather. I also like sharing stories about the students whose lives have changed because they got to go to school in one of the schools my dad started.

My dad works really hard, all day and night all year, and we make sacrifices to help him. My dad is cool because he chose to go down a different path and he's not afraid of big challenges or failing. He didn't have to do that, and could have just worked to get us a big fancy house and stuff like that. But he chose to live a simple life; it was something his heart told him to do. I'm so proud of him.

### When he's away, how are you able to stay connected with him?

We use the phone, and this year we figured out Skype, which is cool because you can see somebody talking to you on the computer. When I was little, we filmed a video before he went overseas, and we watched those every day. In our community, everybody helps us. My teachers especially help me get through it because they're involved in what he's doing. They always ask, "Are you okay?" I feel like I have to be responsible when Dad is gone, because my mom can't do everything on her own. My grandma, Lila, lives a block away, and my other grandma, Jerene, is nearby in Yellowstone Park half the year. They are both incredible grandmas, and help us out.

I think it's hard though. Khyber doesn't express himself much. Like he doesn't say, "I miss Dad," and keeps it inside.

Then when a small thing happens, he sometimes turns it into a dramatic thing, and we kind of know it's his way of saying, "I'm not happy, I want my dad home." And so I feel like my family has gotten closer from that. I'm not saying it's a good thing; I'm saying it's definitely helped us get through harder times.

*So, describe the day your dad leaves for Pakistan or for a fund-raiser for the Central Asia Institute. What is that like for you?*

Well, usually we get up, and we don't want him to go, and we hug him like crazy, and then we'll probably cry a little bit, not a ton. Then we'll go to school and we'll come home and he'll be there because he misses his flights the first day. That's why we don't cry that dramatically, because we know he's going to be there when we get home. And then the next day is a lot harder.

It's especially hard on his U.S. trips. When he's in Pakistan, he's gone for a long time, and we adjust. We say good-bye, he goes, he comes home, and we're happy. When he's on trips in the United States, it's: "I'm gonna go here for three days, then I'll be home a day, and then leave for a week." That's the hardest one for us, because he's home, then gone, and it's like, "I'm home, I love you, but I gotta go now." It hurts, because we wish he wouldn't have to do this so much.

Lots of people recognize my dad in airports, stores, parks, and everywhere. No place is totally private, and they're like,

Amira with Mansur, a Frontier Corps soldier; 1997

"Oh, my God, you're Greg Mortenson," and it gets really annoying after a while. Even when we go to buy bread at Joe's Parkway Store, or get an ice-cream cone, it's like we're there for sixty minutes more than we need to be. It gets chaotic when people treat my dad like a rock star. But to me he's just a dad and normal dude. I wish people would just understand that when he's home, he's home for us, and we need time alone. Right now it's family time.

*When you go to your school after your dad has left for a big trip, what do the teachers and kids in your class do?*

I have a small school, so everyone knows each other, and they give me hugs. It just helps a lot to know that there's love in many places. My dad gets thousands of requests to speak at schools. So probably the special-est thing is that my own school leaves my dad alone and he is not asked to be anything other than my dad, or give a talk there.

My math teacher recently said to me, "When he is gone, just remember all the good times you've had with him, instead of the bad things like that he's gone or that he's in a dangerous country. Remember the time that you went and got ice cream with him and had a really nice walk, or he came to your birthday."

*When you do think about the scary things, what sorts of things are you thinking about or imagining your dad doing?*

Well, of course, I'm worried about the Taliban and terrorists. My dad's a peacemaker, and some people hate him or are jealous, even in America. He has been threatened to be killed. He was kidnapped in 1996, and he almost missed my birth. But he is a smart person, with an incredible staff who love us like our family. My dad even meets and talks with his enemies. And go figure, he is safe, because he drinks lots of tea and makes friends everywhere. And meeting his staff a bunch of times, it just feels so much better to hand him over to them. There are some pretty amazing people on that staff.

*Like who?*

Well, there's Apo—the old guy, like a grandpa. He's so sweet, loving, and kind. His old house held the record for "biggest toilet hole," that was twenty-eight feet deep. He doesn't talk much, but you can see it that he's really happy to see you. Apo used to feed me sugar cubes when I was little. The first time we went there, my mom was like, "Why does Amira like Apo so much?" Finally my dad caught him sneaking sugar cubes to me, and that's probably why I love sugar even today.

And then there's Sarfraz Khan. Sarfraz is an incredible guy who coordinates everything, who can speak about eight languages, ride a horse like a cowboy, fix a computer, and is a very brave man to help get girls in school in dangerous areas where the Taliban are. And I love him very much. Then there's Faisal Baig, who's like my dad's security guard. He's quiet, but watch out if anyone tries to hurt you or look at you the wrong way. He once nearly killed a man who tried to make a pass at my mom. Then there's Suleman Minhas, who used to be a taxi driver, who is one of my dad's main managers. He's really fun. One time, when I was little, Suleman and Apo were babysitting me, and my parents came back and were like, "Where's Amira?" Just then, Suleman drove by, with Apo holding me out the car window, I had a huge balloon and cotton candy in my arms and was totally happy. Mr. Parvi is another man who has helped my dad out for fifteen years, and he has many beautiful daughters who I am friends with. We're like one big family.

**What do you like best about helping with Pennies for Peace™ and your dad's work? Do you like talking to kids and sharing your experiences with other people?**

I like to see how they react when they hear about kids having to walk three hours to get to school every morning, and get up at four to do their chores, then go to school, walk back, then do more chores.

Compared to them, we are spoiled. I don't mean to call anyone spoiled, but we have so much more than them and we're still picky. I think kids could totally care more. Instead of asking their mom for twenty dollars to go buy this plastic kung fu ninja that came out, they could say, "You know what, maybe I don't need this. Maybe I can buy nothing this time." It's hard for me; I can't do that, either. I really have to try! I think if all of us at least tried to do that, then we'd be definitely more open to the world.

I like talking to kids better than adults. Adults are just like, "She's cute." And kids are like, "I can really do something!" Kids actually even started Pennies for Peace™.

## Really? Tell us a little bit about that.

In 1995, my dad had just been overseas and was trying to raise money to build the first school in Korphe. He did not have much luck, even with famous people and adults. My grandma was a principal at Westside Elementary in River Falls, Wisconsin. She asked him to come speak to her school about his work. He went there without even thinking the kids would help. This fourth-grader named Jeffrey came up afterward, and told my dad he would help, seriously. He said he had a piggy bank at home and was going to empty it out. My dad didn't think much of it at first. But in six weeks, Westside school raised 62,345 pennies! The only check he had ever gotten from an adult was $100, and nothing from all the celebrities he'd asked to pitch in. You know, it was kids who were the first to reach out. I think it's kids who will bring peace to the world also.

Pennies for Peace™ isn't just about raising money for students' supplies in Afghanistan and Pakistan. Kids raise pennies for all kinds of things. My dad says, "Do one good deed every day and the world will be a better place." Just do one good deed, like take out the trash.

### What sorts of questions do you get from American students when you speak to their classes?

First- to fifth-graders ask questions like, "Do they have Game Boys or watch TV?" or "How can we help?" And younger kids often want to know what they eat, or what they play.

They have chores just like we do, but their chores are much more serious—and their lives depend on it. They work for hours in a field, carry water many miles, or take goats and sheep to the mountains to graze and have to watch out for wolves. The kids love to jump rope, hopscotch, play cricket and soccer. But some don't even have a jump rope or ball, so they make up games with sticks and stones. In 2006, I told my dad that all the students should have a little fun and a place to play with recess. He listened to me, and put playgrounds in all the schools. The owner of Gold's Gym helped me raise playground money and donated hundreds of skipping ropes. Playing makes kids happy everywhere, and helps teach kids how to get along.

Kids anywhere can make a difference, whether it's just

picking up trash in their communities, helping an old person, or getting involved with something like Pennies for Peace™. A little help goes a long way.

**What's the most difficult question you've answered when you visit American schools?**

Probably the most difficult question for me to answer is "What's it like to be with kids who are orphans, or starving, or been in war, or refugees who live in a tent?" That's a hard question to answer, because many of us in the United States don't know what that is really like, and it's hard to explain.

**If you were to help students figure out what they could do with their energy to help others, to change the world, to make a difference, what sort of things would you tell them?**

Well, writing letters to kids and having pen pals is probably a big one because they understand that they're just kids and we're equal. And we have brothers and sisters and we do chores around the house and, you know, "I have a cow and you have a dog." It's kind of the same. If we become equals with each other then we won't judge each other, and if we don't judge each other there won't be wars, and if we don't have wars, we'll have hope. And like I said, hope can do anything.

**What do you want to do when you grow up?**

I would love to work with disabled children and music. And 'd love to travel the world, and be like my dad. Of course, I also want to be a singer or go to Broadway. But a singing career is not really enough, and I want to do more than just entertain people. I can sing anytime or anywhere. I'll always get to sing, but you don't always get to spread peace. And I think our generation should be totally dedicated to peace, and not war, and we should make sure every kid in the world can go to school.

*You've had some cool opportunities. Would you tell us about some special people whom you met, because you happen to be Greg Mortenson's daughter?*

I got to meet Oprah Winfrey and Jane Goodall in 2008. I got to "meet" Oprah, unofficially, and she gave me a hug. She really lights up a room, and is making a big difference in the world. Jane Goodall is very kind, sweet, and she really, really cares. She totally inspires me. She's such an amazing person and has dedicated her whole life to science, animals, and even kids with her Roots & Shoots program. Jane is a wise woman, and like so calm. She speaks in a cool British accent. Even though Jane is a celebrity and important, she is so humble and gentle. Jane is cool because she loves everything and everybody.

*What inspires you?*

My mom is the most inspirational person in my life. She's a very "Go and get 'em, girl; be proud of yourself" kind of woman. She is strong, and takes care of us many months every year when my dad is gone. My mom and I are close, like best buddies, and she is fun to hang out with. Sometimes when my dad is away, we get lonesome, and we watch romantic comedies together and share Kleenex tissues for a good cry.

Tyra Banks, I love Tyra Banks. Not only does she host my favorite show, but she's just so enthusiastic about everything, and she's just all like, "You should care." She does it in a nice way like, "This is so much fun." I like Ellen DeGeneres, also, because she dances and sings. She's awesome. I also admire Oprah for helping African kids, and celebrities who work for peace. I mean, yeah, all those women are great people, and we can learn something from all of them. But it's most important to remember that you don't have to be a celebrity to make a difference. There are role models in all our lives.

*So these young women over in Pakistan and Afghanistan, who are their heroes? Do they have women like these women in your life?*

I think education really inspires them. I mean, without education, they wouldn't be where they are today. They wouldn't have the courage to try and make it in today's world. The heroes for the young women in Pakistan are usually their grandmothers, moms, and teachers. And I think that's what makes all of us equal. We all have someone who we look up to, and then we all have someone who looks up to us.

Personally, I look up to them as my heroes, because they go to school, and they're really proud of it. They have the courage to stand up for what they believe in, and not fear some crazy men who want to keep them like slaves or stop them from

Khyber auctions off a painting at a fund-raiser in Chicago; 2008

learning. Not everyone can do that, and that's what makes them so amazing.

### Do you want to share any more of your stories or some of your favorite memories?

I didn't share enough about my brother, who I love very much. Khyber is eight and in third grade. He loves school, and is very smart. He probably knows more history than me, and he is a computer whiz. He's a good brother. We don't fight a lot like some siblings. Of course, we do have arguments, but we usually figure things out without too much of a scene. Probably because we both know how lucky we are to live in the United States, where we have so many choices and wonderful stuff like education, peace, and freedom.

Khyber is a little shy, but has a big heart and loves to be with his friends. Theater helps him gain confidence. He makes good choices, and cares a lot about nature, animals, insects, and people. He hardly eats meat, even though he did not know what a vegetarian meant until last year. I'm proud to be his sister.

### What are some of the things that he says about poverty or the children over in Pakistan and Afghanistan?

Khyber is a sensitive person and like a wise man, which I think is great for a boy his age. He is really bothered by the fact that there are land mines in Afghanistan that are designed to blow up and hurt children. He asks questions like, "Amira, how can we help those kids?" He wants to design a video game

for Pennies for Peace™, which kids would really go for. He likes
to share his money for good things. I think Khyber wants to be
like Dad more than anything in the world, and that makes all
of us proud.

Greg and Khyber Mortenson

# Amira's Photos

The Mortenson family in Montana: Khyber, Greg, Tara, and Amira: 2007

Lila Bishop

Amira (age 3) with Kalash tribal girls in Pakistan: 1999

ira (age 3) carrying at in Pakistan: 1999

Tara Bishop

Tara Bishop

Amira (8 months) plays with friends in Pakistan; 1997

Amira (age 3) with her mom, Tara, at Tisar Village, Pakistan; 1999

GIRLS SCHOOL TISAR (1999)
SPECIAL THANKS TO:
AMERICAN ALPINE CLUB U.S.A

CENTRAL ASIA INSTITUTE U.S.A
zeman MT 59715
Fax: 406 586 9516

Greg Mortenson

"[Pakistan]'s totally different. The last time I went was in the summer of 2007 when I was ten."

Amira in the Deosai Plateau wilderness; 2007

Greg Mortenson

A visit to Hussein's house, Skardu, Pakistan; 2007

Mohammed Nazir

The Chunda Girls School Inauguration: 2007

Greg Mortenson

WELCOME OUR DISTINGUISHED GUESTS
Dr. Greg Mortensen Dr. Tara Mr. Aleem Adil Sheikh
Ms Noor ul din (Advisor) Mr. Mirza Hu

Greg with the Chunda Village elders: 2007

Deirdre Eitel © 2007

Amira, Khyber, and the deputy director of education cut ribbon to open the Chunda Girls School: 2007

Greg Mortenson

"I think [Khyber] wants to be like Dad...and that makes us all proud."

"[My dad] chose to go down a different path... it was just something his heart told him to do. I'm so proud of him."

"My mom is a very 'go get 'em, be proud of yourself' kind of person."

Amira with Chunda schoolgirls; 2007

*Tara Bishop*

"I didn't want the kids to feel like I was more important than them because I'm not. I'm just a kid....Kids anywhere can make a difference... a little help goes a long ways."

Promote Literacy...
Promote Peace

A Pennies for Peace™ fund-raiser in Chicago

*Tara Bishop*

"When they write they have hope, and when they have hope, they can accomplish anything."

Tara Bishop

"Jane Goodall's very kind, very sweet, and she really cares.... She's such an amazing person and she's dedicated her whole life to science and animals."

Jane Goodall visits the Mortensons in Montana; 2008

Tara Bishop

Amira and Khyber sell lemonade to raise money for Pennies for Peace™; 2006

Tara Bishop

Amira sings the song
"Three Cups of Tea"
in Pakistan: 2007

Greg Mortenson

"Just hearing the voice of hope that anyone can give
them…just saying, 'If you try hard enough, you will
become what you want to be.'"

# Time Line

**1947**

August 14      Pakistan declares independence.

**1957**

December      Greg Mortenson born in Minnesota.

**1958**

March      Greg and family move to Usambara Mountains, Tanganyika (now Tanzania), Africa, when he is three months old.

**1959**

June      Greg's sister Sonja born in Tanzania.

**1960**      Greg and family move to Moshi, Tanzania, on south slopes of Mount Kilimanjaro.

**1963**

May      Tara Bishop, Greg's wife, born in Maryland.

July      Greg's sister Kari born in Minnesota.

**1969**

June      Greg's sister Christa born in Tanzania.

**1972**      Greg and family leave Africa and move to Minnesota.

**1974**      Greg's sister Christa is diagnosed with epilepsy at age four.

# Three Cups of Tea

**1975**

June            Greg graduates from Ramsey High School in Roseville, Minnesota, and joins the U.S. Army four days later.

**1977–1979**      Greg attends Concordia College in Minnesota and plays on the national champion football team.

**1979**             The Soviet Army invades Afghanistan and stays for nine years.

**1980**

September     Greg's dad, Dempsey Mortenson, dies of cancer in his late forties.

**1983**             Greg graduates from the University of South Dakota and moves to Black Hills, South Dakota, to work as an emergency room nurse.

**1985**             Greg moves to Indianapolis, Indiana.

**1988**             Greg moves to Minnesota to live with his sister Christa for a year.

**1992**

July 24       Greg falls on Mount Sill in California and is injured; Greg's sister Christa dies the same morning.

**1993**

June            Greg begins his K2 climb.

September     Greg gets lost hiking out of K2, arrives in Korphe.

## 1993

October — Greg returns to the United States, and begins raising money for the Korphe School.

## 1994

August — Dr. Jean Hoerni hears of Greg's work, and sends him money to build the Korphe School.

October — The Taliban start their campaign and attack a United Nations compound in Afghanistan.

October–December — Greg returns to Pakistan to buy materials to build the Korphe School.

## 1995

Spring — Westside Elementary School in River Falls, Wisconsin, collects 62,345 pennies to help students in Pakistan.

Summer — Greg and the Korphe villagers build the Braldu River bridge in Korphe.

Fall — Greg returns to the United States, visits Dr. Hoerni, and shows him a picture of the Korphe bridge.

September 13 — Greg meets Tara Bishop in San Francisco. They get married six days later.

October — Greg travels to Pakistan to begin building Korphe's school.

November — Greg returns to the United States, where he and Tara spend Thanksgiving with Dr. Hoerni, and start the Central Asia Institute.

## 1996

| | |
|---|---|
| May | Greg returns to Pakistan, as director of the CAI. |
| Summer | Construction starts on Korphe School. |
| August | Greg is kidnapped and held for eight days in Waziristan, Pakistan. |
| September | Greg and Tara's daughter, Amira Eliana Mortenson, is born at their home in Bozeman, Montana. |
| December | The Korphe School is completed. |

## 1997

| | |
|---|---|
| January | Dr. Jean Hoerni dies of leukemia in Seattle, Washington. |
| August 7 | Al Qaeda bombs the U.S. embassies in Tanzania and Kenya, killing 258 people. |
| Summer | Greg, Tara, and Amira Mortenson visit Pakistan for the Korphe School opening. |

## 1999

| | |
|---|---|
| May | Fighting breaks out between Pakistan and Afghanistan. Many refugees arrive in Skardu. |
| June | Pakistan detonates its first nuclear bomb. |
| Summer and Fall | Greg, Tara, and Amira spend several months in Pakistan. Gultori war refugee girls' school is built in Skardu. |

**2000**                Greg's wife, Tara, receives her Ph.D. in clinical
                        psychology.

July                    Greg and Tara's son, Khyber Bishop
                        Mortenson, is born at home in Bozeman,
                        Montana.

**2001**

September 11            Al Qaeda uses hijacked commercial passenger
                        jets to bomb the World Trade towers in New
                        York City and the Pentagon in Washington,
                        D.C., and one plane crashes in Pennsylvania.

September 12            Greg finds out about the World Trade Center
                        and Pentagon bombings while in Pakistan.

September               Greg discovers that Haji Ali has died.

October                 The United States and a military coalition of
                        eighteen other countries invade Afghanistan.

October 31              Greg returns to the United States.

Winter                  Greg visits Afghanistan, then Washington,
                        D.C., where he meets with Representative
                        Mary Bono.

**2002**                Greg and the CAI start building girls' schools
                        in Afghanistan.

September               Greg and reporter Kevin Fedarko visit schools
                        in Pakistan.

**2003**

April          The United States invades Iraq.

April 6        *Parade* magazine article about Greg and his work is published.

**2004**

Summer      Greg and CAI begin building schools in Badakshan province in northern Afghanistan.

**2005**

October 8     A massive earthquake in Azad Kashmir, Pakistan, kills over 74,000 people, including 18,000 students in schools, and destroys over 1,600 schools.

November–   Greg visits areas of Pakistan affected by the
December     earthquake and starts tent schools.

**2006**

CAI begins building earthquake-proof schools in Azad Kashmir.

Greg begins visiting schools, sharing how to promote peace through education with students. From 2006 to 2008 he travels to over 200 U.S. cities and visits over 400 schools.

March 30     *Three Cups of Tea* is published by Viking Penguin, and Greg appears on *Good Morning America*.

# 2007

January 30    Penguin Books publishes the paperback edition
              of *Three Cups of Tea*. It becomes a *New York
              Times* best seller.

Summer        Greg and his family visit friends and schools in
              Pakistan.

              The Taliban attacks Lalander School in
              Afghanistan, shutting it down for two days.

# 2008

May           Amira and Khyber Mortenson meet Oprah
              Winfrey and Jane Goodall.

              *Three Cups of Tea* is chosen as required reading
              for intelligence training by the Pentagon and
              U.S. military.

June          Greg and CAI start schools in Kunar province
              in eastern Afghanistan.

# 2009

January       Puffin Books publishes the young readers
              edition of *Three Cups of Tea*.

              Dial publishes *Listen to the Wind*, a picture
              book by Greg Mortenson and Susan Roth.

# Glossary

*Allah*: The Arabic word for God.

*Allah Akbhar*: In Arabic, "God is great." This exclamation can be used in prayer, to praise God, or to express approval, excitement, or happiness.

*Al Qaeda*: A radical Islamic organization which conducts acts of terror, war, and destruction of Western targets all over the world in order to establish a global Islamic civilization.

*amber*: Lumps of fossilized tree sap, often made into jewelry.

*American Himalayan Foundation (AHF)*: A nonprofit organization that works to help people of the Himalayas; www.himalayan-foundation.org.

*Angrezi*: White person or Westerner.

*antibiotic*: Medicine that kills the bacteria that can cause infection or illness.

*artillery*: Large weapons that shoot bombs, rockets, or shells from a tube.

*As-salaam alaikum*: In Arabic, "Peace be with you" or "Peace be upon you." A common greeting.

*avalanche*: A sudden and enormous collapse of snow that roars down a mountain with great force.

**Badakhshan:** Province in northeast Afghanistan.

**Balti:** A tribal group that lives in the Karakoram Mountains in northeast Pakistan.

**board:** A group of people who run an organization, often deciding what kind of work it should do, whom it should hire, and how its money should be spent.

**briefing:** A meeting where important information is shared.

**Central Asia Institute (CAI):** The nonprofit organization that Greg cofounded that builds schools in Afghanistan and Pakistan; www.ikat.org.

**chapatti:** A flat unleavened bread, similar to a pita bread or a tortilla.

**chat-ndo:** A promise.

**Cheezaley:** In Balti, "What the heck!"

**commandhan:** The commander of a local militia; warlord.

**Dari:** The form of the **Farsi** language spoken in Afghanistan.

**dispensary:** A place where medicines and medical supplies are stored and given out to people who need them. Simple medical treatment may also be provided.

**Diwali:** A religious festival, often called the "Festival of Lights," celebrated by Hindus.

**dupatta:** A headscarf worn by girls.

**embassy:** The residence or office of an ambassador, the person sent as the chief representative of his or her own government in another country; the official headquarters of one country's government that is located in another country.

*empower*: To give authority or power to.

*endow*: To give, or give money.

*epilepsy*: A disease that causes seizures.

*expedition*: A journey made by a group of people to explore or accomplish a goal.

*Farsi*: Persian language.

*Feast of Id*: A religious festival, celebrated by Muslims, that marks the end of Ramadan, the month when Muslims fast during the day.

*generator*: A machine that creates electricity.

*GI Bill*: A program that provides money from the government for veterans (soldiers who served in the armed forces) to go to college, university, or a trade school.

*glacier*: A massive, slow-moving river of ice.

*Himalayas*: The mountain range in southern Asia that borders Burma, India, China, Nepal, Tibet, and Pakistan.

*hostel*: A place where travelers or those away from home can stay. A hostel is usually simple and inexpensive.

*House of Representatives*: One of the two houses of the United States Congress, and part of the legislative branch.

*illiterate*: Being unable to read and write.

*infidel*: Someone who does not believe in the same religion as the person using the term.

*initiative*: Taking a first step; getting started.

*Inshallah*: In Arabic, "God willing" or "If God allows it." It is often used to mean that the speaker hopes something will occur or that he or she will be able to accomplish something, but that it is uncertain and God's help and blessing will be needed.

*irrigation channels*: Ditches that bring water to crops.

*Islam*: Means peace in Arabic. A religion based on the teaching of the prophet Mohammed; the world's second-largest religion.

*jirga*: A village council or meeting.

*kafir*: A nonbeliever or infidel.

*Karakoram*: The mountain region that includes K2 and many mountain villages, such as Korphe.

*Kashmir*: The mountainous region bordered by India and Pakistan.

*Kilimanjaro*: An inactive volcano in Tanzania; Africa's tallest mountain at 19,340 feet high.

*Kilimanjaro Christian Medical Centre (KCMC)*: The hospital in Moshi, Tanzania, started by Greg Mortenson's father, Dempsey, in 1971.

*Koran*: The most important religious book in Islam.

*land mine:* An explosive device buried just underground. It will usually explode if it is stepped on, if a car or other vehicle drives over it, or if something made of metal comes nearby.

*lassi:* A drink made with yogurt.

*laudable:* Excellent, worthy of praise.

*ledgers:* Books in which accounts are kept of how much money a business is receiving and spending.

*legacy:* Something left or given after a person dies.

*leukemia:* A cancer of the blood or bone marrow.

*malnutrition:* Damage caused to the body by not eating enough food or not eating the right kinds of healthy food.

*mason:* A skilled worker who builds with stone, brick, and cement.

*media:* Newspapers, books, TV, movies, and other ways of communicating with a large audience.

*medic:* Someone who is trained to give basic medical treatment.

*meningitis:* A disease that attacks the brain, causing high fevers and headaches.

*mosque:* A building in which Muslims worship.

*mullah:* An Islamic religious leader, similar to a priest, rabbi, or minister.

# Three Cups of Tea

*Muslim:* A person who practices Islam.

*nervous system:* The brain and nerves.

*news anchor:* Someone who reads the news on a TV show.

*Nobel Prize:* An award given once a year to a person or group who has done the most or best work in a given field. It is given in the fields of chemistry, economics, medicine, literature, and peace.

*nomad:* A person or tribe who move from place to place, often living in tents and herding animals.

*nonprofit:* A group or organization that purposefully does not make a profit; often describes a charity.

*nurmadhar:* A village chief.

*opium:* An addictive drug made from poppy seeds.

*order:* A group of people who share a religious belief.

*orderly:* Someone without medical training who works in a hospital, doing jobs like moving patients.

*painkillers:* Drugs or medicines that ease pain.

*paiyu cha:* A hot green tea, made with salt, baking soda, goat's milk, and an aged, sour butter churned from yak's milk.

*Pamir Mountains:* A mountain range in Central Asia.

*Pashto:* A language spoken by tribal peoples in the area between Pakistan and Afghanistan; also called Pushto.

*Pennies for Peace*™: A program started in 1995 by school-children to collect pennies for causes, including aiding children in Pakistan and Afghanistan. www.penniesforpeace.org.

*polio*: A serious sickness that can paralyze someone or damage and weaken muscles.

*poverty*: The state of being poor; not having enough food, clean water, shelter, clothing, and money.

*refugees*: People who have been forced to flee their homes because of war, violence, a natural disaster, or another cause.

*rupee*: Money used in Pakistan, India, and other countries. In Pakistan, 1 rupee is worth about 1.5 U.S. cents.

*Sahib*: A respectful way to address a man considered to be important.

*savannah*: A flat grassland.

*seizure*: A sudden attack, often caused by disease. Someone with epilepsy may have serious seizures during which he or she collapses and the muscles jerk uncontrollably.

*shalwar kamiz*: Loose, pajamalike pants and top.

*shell*: An explosive object fired from a large gun, such as the gun on a tank.

*summit*: The top of a mountain.

*Swahili:* The national language of Tanzania. It is spoken in many other African countries as well.

*Tajikistan:* The mountainous country that is north of Afghanistan.

*tenet:* One of a set of important beliefs.

*tomar:* A small medallion given to every child born into the Balti tribe as a badge of courage meant to keep away evil spirits.

*Urdu:* The national language of Pakistan.

*vocational:* Relating to a skill or a trade.

*Wakhi:* The Persian tribal people of northern Pakistan.

*warlord:* A military leader who rules an area by force.

*Waziristan:* A region of western Pakistan located in the Northwest Frontier Province (NWFP).

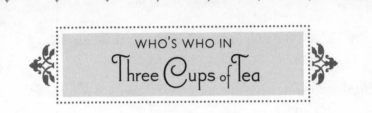

*Akhmalu*: Greg's K2 cook from Khane village in the Hushe Valley.

*Ali, Nargiz*: Friend of Fatima Batool.

*Baig, Faisal*: Greg's bodyguard; from the Charpusan Valley, Pakistan.

*Batool, Fatima*: Young girl who survived her village's bombing and attended the CAI's school for refugees in Skardu.

*Baz, Bashir, Brigadier General*: Officer retired from Pakistan army who helped Greg after the events of September 11, 2001.

*Bergman, Julia*: Librarian at City College in San Francisco, California; former CAI board director.

*bin Laden, Osama*: Saudi Arabian–born leader of Al Qaeda who is now either in hiding or dead.

*Bishop, Lila and Barry*: Tara's parents. Lila has led treks in Nepal and Tibet for decades. Barry was a mountain climber who climbed Mount Everest in 1963. Barry led the department of research and exploration at *National Geographic* for thirty years before his death in 1994.

*Bishop, Tara*: Psychotherapist and Greg Mortenson's wife.

**Bono, Mary:** Republican U.S. Representative from Palm Springs, California.

**Brokaw, Tom:** NBC news anchor who gave Greg his first check in 1993.

**Bullock, James:** San Franscisco cable car driver and surfer; friend of Tara Bishop and Greg Mortenson.

**Changazi, Mohammed:** Tour operator from Skardu.

**Darsney, Scott:** K2 climber from Alaska.

**Faizad, Uzra:** Principal of Durkhani high school in Kabul, Afghanistan.

**Fedarko, Kevin:** Journalist and writer for *Outside* and *Parade* magazines.

**Goodall, Dr. Jane:** English primatologist, ethologist, anthropologist, famous for her forty-five-year study of chimpanzees in Tanzania and widely recognized for her global efforts to protect the chimpanzees. She founded the Jane Goodall Institute, which promotes community-based conservation efforts, and their global youth program, Roots & Shoots.

**Haji Ali:** Greg Mortenson's mentor and village chief of Korphe. He died in 2001.

**Haji Mehdi:** Chief of Askole; demanded bribe from Haji Ali for the Korphe School.

**Haji Mirza:** Chief of Kot Langarkhel; Greg was kidnapped while with him.

*Hillary, Edmund, Sir:* (1919–2008) The first person, with Tenzing Norgay, to climb Mount Everest. Hillary, from New Zealand, and Norgay, a guide from Nepal, made their historic summit in 1953.

*Hoerni, Jean, Dr.:* (1924–1997) A silicon transistor pioneer and co-founder, with Greg Mortenson, of Central Asia Institute.

*Hussain, Aziza:* The first healthcare worker in Zuudkhan.

*Hussein:* Korphe's first schoolteacher, and father of Tahira, Jahan's friend.

*Jahan:* Granddaughter of Haji Ali and the first educated woman in Korphe.

*Janjungpa:* K2 porter from Khane village in the Hushe Valley.

*Kais:* Greg's translator in Afghanistan; helped Greg escape a firefight by hiding him under goatskins.

*Khan, Abdul Rashid:* The warlord who controlled the Kirghiz area of Afghanistan.

*Khan, Mohammed Aslam:* Village chief of Hushe, where Greg built a school; very educated.

*Mazur, Dan:* K2 climber from Washington who reached K2's summit in 1993.

*McCown, George:* San Francisco Bay Area businessman and staunch CAI supporter who was with Greg in Pakistan on 9/11.

*McCown, Karen:* Wife of George, educator and CAI board director.

# Three Cups of Tea

**Minhas, Suleman:** Former taxi driver and Central Asia Institute's operations manager in Pakistan.

**Mortenson, Amira:** Greg Mortenson and Tara Bishop's older child.

**Mortenson, Christa:** Younger sister of Greg Mortenson, who passed away when she was twenty-three in 1992.

**Mortenson, Irvin "Dempsey" and Jerene:** Greg's parents. Jerene is an educator and founder of the International School in Moshi, Tanzania. Dempsey founded the Kilimanjaro Christian Medical Centre and died in 1980.

**Mortenson, Greg:** Cofounder of Central Asia Institute and co-author of *Three Cups of Tea*.

**Mortenson, Khyber:** Greg Mortenson and Tara Bishop's younger child.

**Mother Teresa:** (1910–1997) Catholic nun born in Albania who set up the Daughters of Charity in Calcutta, India. She won the Nobel Peace Prize in 1979 for helping desperately poor, sick, and dying people.

**Mouzafer:** Greg's K2 porter.

**Omar, Amir (Mullah):** Afghan Taliban leader, now in hiding.

**Parvi, Ghulam:** Central Asia Institute's Skardu-based manager and accountant.

**Pratt, Jonathan:** English climber who reached the summit of K2 in 1993.

**Razak, Apo:** Central Asia Institute worker and friend of Amira Mortenson, and the Mortenson family.

*Risvi, Syed Abbas:* Head religious Imam in Northern Pakistan.

*Sakina:* Haji Ali's wife (died 2001).

*Sen, Amartya:* Nobel Peace Prize–winning economist (1998) from Harvard University whose work focuses on education and redefining poverty.

*Shah, Abdul:* The watchman at Greg's hotel in Rawalpindi.

*Shah, Zahir:* (1914–2007) King of Afghanistan from 1933 to 1973, who fled to Italy in 1973 when he was overthrown in a military coup. He later returned to Afghanistan, until his death in 2007.

*Shakeela:* Mohammed Aslam Khan's daughter, and first girl to go to high school in her village.

*Syed, Kishwar:* Pakistani owner of the shop where Greg learned to use a computer.

*Tahira:* Classmate of Jahan, daughter of Master Hussein, Korphe's teacher.

*Takhi, Sher:* The mullah of Korphe.

*Twaha:* Haji Ali's son and father of Jahan.

*Vaughan, Tom:* Climber who wrote an article about Greg in the American Himalayan Foundation's newsletter.

*Wilson, Jennifer:* Jean Hoerni's wife.

*Yasmine:* Parvi's fifteen-year-old daughter; received one of the Central Asia Institute's first scholarships.

## READERS GUIDE

### DISCUSSION QUESTIONS

1. Why does Greg decide to build a school for the children of Korphe? In whose honor does Greg intend to build the school? If you wanted to honor someone special to you, what would you most like to accomplish and for whom?

2. How does Greg feel when he returns to the United States with the school still not built? If Greg had tried to build a school in a poor part of the United States, how would his experience have been similar or different?

3. What is important about Greg's friendships with Haji Ali, Twaha, and other people he meets as his schoolbuilding effort grows? Do Haji Ali and Twaha behave as you might have imagined villagers in Pakistan behaving before you read this book? How do the descriptions of Greg's friendships with these individuals help readers feel more connected to the Pakistani and Afghan people in the book?

4. Chapter 19 recounts the events of September 11, 2001, and concludes with a speech by Muslim leader Syed Abbas at a CAI school inauguration celebration. How did reading Syed Abbas's speech make you feel? Did you find other quotations in the book from Muslim leaders, schoolchildren, or others surprising, informative, or reassuring? Explain your answers.

5. Amira Mortenson describes the many sacrifices her family has made so that her father, Greg, can continue to help the people of central Asia. Do you think you could make such sacrifices? Why or why not? What do you think sounds most

exciting about Amira's life? What seems most challenging?

6. Do you think the main message of *Three Cups of Tea* can be understood as "education means hope"? What is the most important lesson you personally have learned from reading this book? Explain your answer.

## RESEARCH & WRITING ACTIVITIES

1. The foreward to *Three Cups of Tea* is written by Jane Goodall. Learn more about Dr. Goodall's humanitarian and conservation efforts. Compile your research in a short report, and be sure to include a paragraph describing the connections you see between the efforts of Jane Goodall and those of Greg Mortenson.

2. Experience life as a Korphe villager. Reread early passages in the book in which Greg describes the children studying outdoors, the homes and customs of the people, and other aspects of the community he comes to love. With friends or classmates, try having school outside, keeping quiet and focused while writing with sticks in the dirt. Spend a day without using the computer, car, or telephone. Afterward, discuss the challenges and possible benefits of such a way of life.

3. What does school mean to you? Create a brochure welcoming new students to your school. Include a map, lists of teachers and recommended classes, and a short essay explaining what makes your school special. Create a drawing, poem, sculpture, or other piece of creative artwork reflecting your feelings about school and learning. Make a list of your future plans, noting how education plays a role in achieving some or all of your goals.

4. As he works to build schools and improve lives, Greg learns about Central Asian cultures. Brainstorm a list of the cultural discoveries you made while reading this book, such as the notion that after sharing "three cups of tea" with someone, you become family. Afterward, discuss the similarities you see between items on your list and Western cultural customs. Has your understanding of Central Asia changed after reading this book?

5. Make a difference. Go online to learn more about Pennies for Peace™ at www.penniesforpeace.org or research another charitable organization. Encourage your school or community to join in such an effort by making informative posters about your charity, speaking to school or community groups (as Greg Mortenson does), and sharing examples of how other kids have made a real difference and inspired you to help make your world better.

6. Visit the Central Asia Institute online at www.ikat.org to learn more about the organization's accomplishments and future projects, Pennies for Peace™, and *Three Cups of Tea*. Write a letter to Greg Mortenson telling him what reading his book has meant to you. Or write a letter to a friend or to your school's or your local newspaper recommending the book as an especially important read for kids today.

*Greg Mortenson's remarkable story is also a picture book!*

# LISTEN TO THE WIND

The Story of Dr. Greg and
*Three Cups of Tea*
by Greg Mortenson
and Susan L. Roth
collages by Susan L. Roth

The story of how Greg Mortenson helped Korphe build a school is now perfect for reading aloud. Told in the voice of Korphe's children, this story illuminates the humanity and culture of Pakistan in gorgeous collage, while sharing a riveting example of how one person can change thousands of lives.

The book also includes an epilogue full of real-life photographs, explains the work of Dr. Greg and his Central Asia Institute to date, and includes information on how kids can get involved in helping their peers around the world gain access to education.

ISBN: 978-0-8037-3058-8

David Oliver Re

# What is Pennies for Peace™?

Pennies for Peace™ is a service-learning program of Central Asia Institute in which students and kids just like you, across the country and around the world, learn about Pakistan and Afghanistan through Pennies for Peace™ and discover that they can create global change. Central Asia Institute has been building schools and offering children hope for a better future since 1993. When you participate in a Pennies for Peace™ campaign, you join tens of thousands of students around the world who share your vision and dedication to empower communities through education in remote regions of Pakistan and Afghanistan.

# Why pennies?

The penny, one percent of a dollar, is essentially worthless in the United States. In Pakistan and Afghanistan, however, a penny buys a pencil and empowers a child to read and write. Education is the most powerful force to give hope and create change. It can create communities and nations where people have more opportunities and live better, healthier lives.

Povy Kendall Atc

> *"When I look into the eyes of children in Afghanistan and Pakistan, I see my own children. I want my own kids and their counterparts to live in peace, but that will not happen unless we give them alternatives to the cycle of terrorism and war."*

—GREG MORTENSON, FOUNDER OF PENNIES FOR PEACE™
AND EXECUTIVE DIRECTOR OF CENTRAL ASIA INSTITUTE

# How can I help?

You can find out more about our program at www.penniesforpeace.org. The Web site has links to our tool kit, which is designed to help you implement your own Pennies for Peace™ campaign and penny drive! If you choose to participate in a Pennies for Peace™ campaign, please fill out the interactive registration form on the Web site before you begin your penny drive.

Once you've registered, establish a time frame for your campaign. See how many pennies you can raise in two or three months! Visit our Web site www.penniesforpeace.org to find suggestions to incorporate cultural education into your campaign, and start looking for good places to put your coin containers. You can also think of other ways to raise pennies. Be creative! Start a lemonade stand, ask a local business to become a sponsor for your campaign, or call your local newspaper and explain how you are changing the world with your Pennies for Peace™ drive.

Ali Thonson

Greg Mortenson

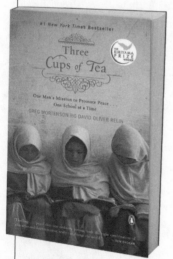